Topics in Modern History Series

GENERAL EDITOR

Ivor D. Astley, B.Sc. *(Econ.),* A.C.P.

Headmaster, Hardley Secondary School, Hampshire

The Growth of Modern Russia
The United Nations
Man and the Atom
The Wind of Change in Africa
The Rise of the U.S.A.
The Trade Union Story
Working-class and Democratic Movements
The Rise of Communist China
Healthy Cities
The First World War
The Second World War

L. F. HOBLEY

The First World War

When can their glory fade?
O the wild charge they made!
All the world wonder'd.

Alfred, Lord Tennyson

There is many a boy here today
who looks on war as all glory, but,
boys, it is all hell.

W. T. Sherman

He had fallen forward and lay on the earth as though
sleeping. Turning him over one saw that he could not have
suffered long; his face had an expression of calm, as
though almost glad the end had come.

E. M. Remarque (*All Quiet on The Western Front*)

BLACKIE GLASGOW AND LONDON

BLACKIE & SON LIMITED
BISHOPBRIGGS . GLASGOW
5 FITZHARDINGE STREET
LONDON W1H 0DL

ISBN   0 216 87210 3 *Educ. Ed.*
ISBN   0 216 88981 2 *Gen. Ed.*

First Published 1971

Printed in Great Britain
by Robert Cunningham & Sons Ltd., Alva

Preface

One of the main aims of this series is to bring history up to date. Unfortunately too many pupils leave our schools with little knowledge of the contemporary world or recent history. Surveys have shown that, for the majority, studies in history ended with the First World War.

In 1963 the Secondary Schools Examinations Council recognized the difficulties of teaching near contemporary history, but also made the point that ... *it is generally accepted that the historian has a special, though not an exclusive, duty to lend significance to the contemporary scene with pupils who are about to join a wider community.*[1]

Many of us have welcomed the chances that the new CERTIFICATE OF SECONDARY EDUCATION EXAMINATION presents—including an opportunity to extend the time-span and thus bring into our syllabus topics which are of relevance, and aid the understanding of the world which awaits the new citizens.

At a Conference of History Teachers in London in 1963, publishers were urged to meet a real need for reasonably-priced *Topic* books—which could more easily be up-to-date than the conventional textbooks. They could also meet other needs by covering subjects of present-day importance. This series has accepted the challenge. The result is a new series of topic books specially written for a better understanding of 'the world today'.

The speed of change in our world is such that even if we reach the end of the Second World War in our syllabus, we are terminating our studies at a point which represents a very different world to most of our readers. The NEWSOM Report reminds us that even in 1945 ... *The first atomic bombs had only just been exploded; Everest and not the moon was still the summit to be reached.*[2]

Of course, even when dealing with new problems, with modern and emerging nations, etc., we find that the 'roots' go deep. The

[1] *C. S. E. Bulletin No.* 1 (H.M.S.O.)   [2] *Half Our Future* (H.M.S.O.)

topic books must retrace the steps for the story to make sense.

We believe that the first essential is a clear, readable story—the essence of history; secondly, that the series should also provide useful source material—with suggestions for further reading and discussion.

★   ★   ★   ★   ★

More than half a century ago 'The Great War' ended, in 1918. It had been the worst war in the history of mankind—with enormous costs in lives lost and maimed, wasted resources and opportunities, and destruction on a vast scale. Tragically, as President Wilson of the U.S.A. foresaw, it did not prove to be as men hoped 'the war to end wars'. The fact that it is now referred to as the *First* World War is a final bitter irony.

The character of war had changed. Millions were now involved. A few decades before, Tennyson had praised the unquestioning attitude of the 'gallant six hundred' who rode gloriously to their death in *The Charge of the Light Brigade*. Now there could be 60,000 casualties in a single action. There was equal heroism on both sides but few could foresee in 1914 the horrifying developments in warfare. Men were sacrificed in hopeless frontal assaults, mutilated by explosives, drowned in mud and choked with gas . . . 'Glory' seemed an inappropriate word . . . Altogether there were more than 37 million casualties at the end of the war.

In this book Mr. Hobley tells briefly the story of the First World War, and in the Documentary sections gives fuller details of what people on the home and battle fronts felt in the traumatic years 1914–18.

I. D. A.

Contents

Acknowledgments

The author and publisher make grateful acknowledgment to the following for permission to include illustrations as detailed below:

RADIO TIMES HULTON PICTURE LIBRARY
Kaiser William II (p. 3) *1st Dreadnought* (p. 12) *Oxford St.* (p. 5) *Boy soldiers* (p. 34) *Joffre* (p. 39) *Refugees* (p. 40) *British Tommies* (p. 47) *Enlistment poster* (p. 51) *Going over the top* (pp. 58–9) *Zeppelin* (p. 64) *Howitzer crew* (p. 66) *French recruits* (p. 72) *Women factory workers* (p. 79) *Marching to the Front* (p. 80) *Tanks* (p. 81) *Passchendaele ridge* (p. 87) *Russian soldiers deserting* (p. 88) *U-boat* (p. 90) *Sir Douglas Haig* (p. 97) *'Big Four'* (p. 104) *Armistice celebration* (p. 108)

ULLSTEIN BILDERDIENST
Francis Ferdinand's tunic (p. 17) *German students enlisting* (p. 18) *Ludendorff* (p. 36) *German trenches* (p. 46) *Christmas in the trenches* (p. 55) *Gas attack victims* (pp. 62–3) *Signing of Rumanian peace treaty* (p. 76)

THE IMPERIAL WAR MUSEUM
Admiral Beatty (p. 49) *HMS Lion* (p. 75)

THE GLASGOW HERALD *Troops at bayonet practice* (p. 30)

THE PUBLIC RECORD OFFICE *The Treaty of London* (p. 25)

'PUNCH' *Townsend cartoon of German invasion of Belgium* (p. 21)

'THE ILLUSTRATED LONDON NEWS'
Civilian food shortages in Germany and Austria-Hungary (p. 82)

The author and publisher make grateful acknowledgment to all authors and publishers of works from which extracts have been quoted, and to the following who have given their kind permission:

THE FIRST BEAVERBROOK FOUNDATION for an extract from *War Memoirs* by David Lloyd George.

ERNEST BENN LTD. for *Five Souls* by W. N. Ewer.

MLLE. M. BONNET for an extract from *The History of the Russian Revolution* by Leon Trotsky.

HAROLD OWEN ESQ. for an extract from *Dulce et Decorum Est* by Wilfred Owen.

THE ROYAL INSTITUTE OF INTERNATIONAL AFFAIRS for an extract from *A History of Peace Conference of Paris* by H. W. V. Temperley.

PROF. G. P. WELLS for extracts from *The Outline of History* by H. G. Wells.

NATIONALISM

In the early twentieth century there were six countries in Europe which, on account of their population, size, wealth and industrial strength, and consequent military or naval strength, were known as 'Great Powers'. They were: Austria–Hungary, France, Germany, Great Britain, Italy and Russia. Outside Europe there were only two countries which were considered to have similar status—Japan and the United States of America.

There was great rivalry between the European Great Powers in trade, in gaining colonies in other parts of the world, in influencing smaller countries, and in general matters of prestige.

This rivalry led to the growth of a spirit of nationalism, of a very strong feeling of loyalty to their country by the great majority of its citizens. Everywhere people were becoming more and more proud of their country. They loved their country; they were ready to work for it and to die for it.

When they were told that their country was in danger, they were ready to fight for it. More than this, they were prepared to do for their country things they would not think of doing for themselves. Men who were honest and kindly in dealing with other people in everyday life, who would never lie, cheat or steal for their own benefit, were quite glad to do these things on behalf of their country. 'My country, right or wrong', they said.

The governments of countries were therefore ready to cheat one another, to upset one another's trade, to deceive and spy upon one another. They made secret treaties with one another, and no country could be quite sure that others which appeared to be friendly were not double-crossing it and making secret agreements with its enemies or rivals.

There was therefore much fear and mistrust, and each country raised a large army or navy, or both. Most countries had a system of

conscription: every fit man had to become a soldier or serve in the navy for at least two years, so that there would always be plenty of trained men who could be called up if war broke out.

THE GREAT POWERS

The Great Powers varied greatly in size and strength (see chart on p. 112).

Austria–Hungary was known as the 'Dual Monarchy'. It consisted of a combination of the Austrian and Hungarian peoples who ruled over a large territory inhabited by several other nationalities besides their own. The Emperor of Austria was also the King of Hungary. Austria and Hungary each had its own parliament, but a joint government controlled the army, navy and foreign policy, over which the Emperor and his military advisers had complete control. The subject races in Austria–Hungary included several million Czechs, Slovaks, Serbs, Croats, Rumanians and Poles. There was much discontent, and the Czechs, Slovaks, Croats and Poles wanted their independence. The Serbs and Rumanians wanted to be free to join their fellow people in the independent Serbia and Rumania beyond the Austro–Hungarian borders. The inclusion of these subject peoples in the large Austro–Hungarian army weakened it considerably. Austria–Hungary had no overseas empire, and only a small navy.

France was a republican democracy, ruled by a parliament for which all men had the right to vote. The economy of the country was well balanced between a fairly prosperous peasantry, who produced most of the country's food, and a thriving and efficient industry. France had a very large overseas empire, a large, well-trained army and a navy big enough to guard communications with the colonies in many parts of the world.

Germany was highly industrialized, and was rapidly increasing her population, her output of manufactures and her international trade. German workers were protected from poverty in old age, and from sickness and unemployment by a national insurance scheme introduced by the great German statesman Bismarck.

There was a German parliament called the *Reichstag* and most men had the right to vote for it, but the main decisions of government were made by the Kaiser, William II, and his advisers. Little notice was taken of the *Reichstag* in such matters as foreign policy.

Kaiser William II on manoeuvres with his army

The Kaiser had no liking for democracy. 'My trust is placed in the army,' he said. The German army was the most powerful and efficient in the world. Next the Kaiser wanted a powerful navy, and this was greatly strengthened in the early twentieth century.

Germany had entered late in the race for empire; Bismarck had not thought that overseas colonies were of much advantage. Then, in the 1880s had come a change, and Germany acquired colonies in Africa and the Pacific, but they were not a source of great strength or wealth. Germany saw the vast empires of Britain, France and Russia and felt that she had been done out of her rights to a share in such possessions.

Italy was barely powerful enough to be considered as a great power. She had become a united country only in the latter half of the nineteenth century. Her industrial development was only just beginning, and most of her people were very poor peasants. She too had come late into the race for empire, and her colonies in Africa were of little value.

Russia was the largest and most populous country in Europe, and the Russian Empire included an even larger area in northern and central Asia. Most of her people were miserably poor peasants, but in a few large cities, such as St. Petersburg and Moscow, large-scale industry was developing rapidly in the early twentieth century, largely financed by French capital. Here the industrial workers became very dissatisfied with the Russian system of government.

After attempts at revolution in 1905, the Tsar Nicholas II set up a sort of parliament called the *Duma*, but he dismissed it when it criticized the government. In 1907 only wealthy people were allowed to vote for the *Duma*, and the Tsar and his ministers were able to govern as they wished. Russia had a huge army, but it was poorly equipped. She had no overseas colonies, her huge empire being in one vast, compact block.

Great Britain had the largest overseas empire, the largest merchant fleet and the largest navy in the world. She was the only European Great Power that did not conscript her manpower for the army, which was small but well trained. Most of it was stationed in various parts of the empire. Her navy was needed to defend the empire which was scattered throughout the world, and she always tried to keep the navy at least equal to the combined naval forces of any two other powers.

Britain was highly industrialized, but in the early twentieth century there was much discontent among the industrial workers who felt that they were not getting a fair share of their country's prosperity and wealth.

The *U.S.A.* was growing rapidly in population, industry and wealth. Every year large numbers of people from various European countries emigrated there. The U.S.A. was a democracy, and was ruled by a parliament called the Congress. She regarded herself as the protector of the rest of the Americas, and warned all other countries not to interfere. This policy had been expressed a century earlier in the Monroe Doctrine. She did not wish to become mixed up in the quarrels of Europe. She had no conscript army.

Japan was ruled by an emperor and a parliament, but the emperor rnd his ministers, particularly the heads of the army and navy, were the real governing force. She had a very up-to-date army, navy and system of education, modelled on those of Europe and America. She had defeated Russia in 1905 and was building up a Japanese Empire by trying to extend her influence over much of eastern Asia. She was also strengthening herself against possible encroachments into her empire by any other Great Power.

These were the Great Powers who dominated the rest of the world, always scheming to increase their own wealth and power.

They bullied the weaker countries, bluffed one another, and made or unmade alliances when it suited them. Sometimes they made threats which could easily have led to war, but they protested that they did not want war. All, however, were determined to be on the winning side should war break out, so they built up their armaments and kept spies in foreign countries to find out the strength and weakness of possible enemies. Only the U.S.A., with vast natural resources and safely separated from the others by thousands of miles of ocean, took little part in these activities.

Oxford Street, 1909

Documentary One

Germany

Germany took up the organisation of scientific research and of the application of scientific method to industrial and social development with such a faith and energy as no other community had ever shown before.

Throughout all this period of the armed peace she was reaping and sowing afresh and reaping again the harvests of freely disseminated knowledge. She grew swiftly to become a great manufacturing and trading power; her steel output outran the British; in a hundred new fields of production and commerce . . . and in endless novel processes, she led the world. . . . And Germany also led the way in many forms of social legislation.

But this scientific organising spirit was only one of the two factors that made up the new German Empire. The other factor was the Hohenzollern monarchy. . . . In the head of this fine new modern state there sat no fine modern brain to guide it to a world predominance in world service, but an old spider lusting for power.

German historical teaching became an immense systematic falsification of the human past. . . . All other nations were represented as incompetent and decadent; the Prussians were the leaders and regenerators of mankind. The young German read this in his school-books, heard it in church . . . had it poured into him with passionate conviction by his professor.

From THE OUTLINE OF HISTORY by H. G. Wells (Cassell)

Germany felt like a giant striving to burst the bonds which confined him, but look where he would he found that all the most desirable portions of the earth had already been parcelled out. It was right that he should have a share in the earth, but he came too late upon the scene. In all quarters it was the British Empire which seemed to bar his advance. Even France, with a stationary population, managed to secure more colonies than Germany in the years since 1870.

From LIONS LED BY DONKEYS by P. A. Thompson (Werner Laurie)

Russia

While all the world to the west of her was changing rapidly, Russia throughout the nineteenth century changed very slowly. At the end of the nineteenth century she was still a Grand Monarchy . . . standing on a basis of barbarism. . . . The Russian moujik (peasant) was supposed to worship and revere his Tsar and to love and serve a gentleman. . . . The upper classes were as much beyond the sympathy of the lower as a different species of animal.

From THE OUTLINE OF HISTORY by H. G. Wells (Cassell)

Nationalism and patriotism

. . . the nation-state structure, far from being able to prevent war, is the only and ultimate cause of the recurrent international wars.

From THE ANATOMY OF PEACE by Emery Reves (Penguin)

Throughout the nineteenth century . . . there has been a great working up of this nationalism in the world. . . . Nationalism was taught in schools, emphasised by newspapers, preached and mocked and sung into men. It became a monstrous cant which darkened all human affairs.

From THE OUTLINE OF HISTORY by H. G. Wells (Cassell)

Real patriotism, real love of one's country has no relationship whatsoever to the fetishism of the sovereign nation-states. Real patriotism can have but one single purpose: to protect one's own country, one's own people from the devastation of war. As war is the direct result of the nation-state structure, and as modern aerial and mechanised warfare indiscriminately destroys women, children, cities and farms, the nation-state is Enemy No. 1 of patriotism.

From THE ANATOMY OF PEACE by Emery Reves (Penguin)

THE BALKAN STATES

The strongest rivalries were between Austria–Hungary and Russia, Germany and France, and Germany and Britain.

Both Austria–Hungary and Russia wanted to increase their influence in the Balkans. For centuries Russia had been hoping to obtain an ocean port which would not be frozen in the winter. The most convenient one was Constantinople, at which she had been casting envious eyes, for it commanded the Bosphorus and the Dardanelles, the straits leading to the Mediterranean.

Russia had already absorbed a great deal of what had been the northern part of the Turkish Empire, and that had brought her within striking distance of the port. Her policy now was aimed at securing the 'freedom of the Straits' under a weak Turkey, while she dominated the small states of the Balkans. Ultimately, she hoped, Constantinople would come into her own possession. Meanwhile it was natural for Russia to pose as the champion and protector of the Balkan states as most of their peoples were of the Slav race, to which the Russians also belonged.

Along Russia's flank, however, was Austria–Hungary, who also had ambitions in the Balkans, and who, with German support, was threatening to cut across Russia's line of advance. Austria's policy was to maintain and strengthen Turkey, as a defence against Russia and the Slavs generally, and to keep the Balkan states as small, weak and divided as possible. Austria already ruled over some Balkan peoples, and in 1908 she took advantage of a revolution in Turkey to annex the Balkan provinces of Bosnia and Herzgovina. Austria then contained more Serbs than the kingdom of Serbia itself, and her aim was to keep Serbia small and unimportant; if possible, to suppress Serbia altogether.

Russia accordingly made Serbia her special *protegé*, and there was frequent friction between her and Austria, especially when Serbia encouraged the Serbs and other South Slavs in the Austro-Hungarian empire to revolt.

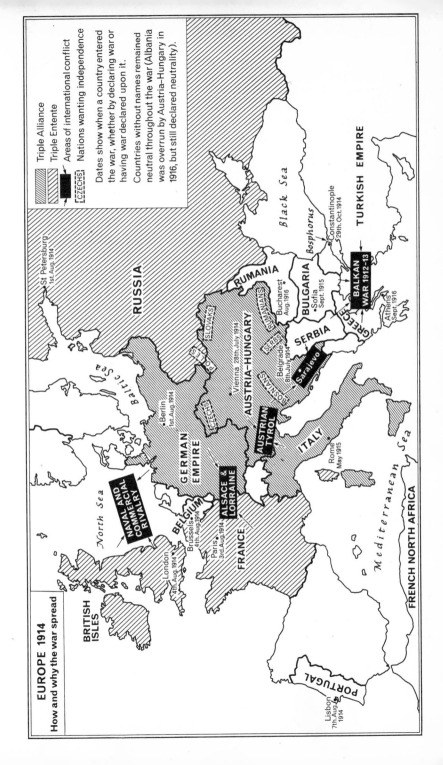

EUROPE 1914
How and why the war spread

Triple Alliance
Triple Entente
Areas of international conflict
Nations wanting independence

Dates show when a country entered the war, whether by declaring war or having war declared upon it.

Countries without names remained neutral throughout the war (Albania was overrun by Austria–Hungary in 1916, but still declared neutrality).

CZECHS

RUSSIA

St Petersburg
1st Aug.1914

Black Sea

Bosphorus

Constantinople
29th.Oct.1914

TURKISH EMPIRE

BALKAN WAR 1912-13

Bulgaria
Sofia
Sept.1915

RUMANIA
Bucharest
Aug.1916

RUMANIANS

SLOVAKS

POLES

Vienna 28th.July 1914

AUSTRIA–HUNGARY

SERBS

Belgrade
8th.July 1914

SERBIA

BOSNIANS

Sarajevo

GREECE
Athens
Sept.1916

Baltic Sea

Berlin
1st.Aug.1914

CZECHS

GERMAN EMPIRE

AUSTRIAN TYROL

ITALY
Rome
May 1915

NAVAL AND COMMERCIAL RIVALRY

North Sea

BRITISH ISLES

London
4th.Aug.1914

BELGIUM
Brussels
4th.Aug.1914

ALSACE & LORRAINE

Paris
3rd.Aug.1914

FRANCE

Mediterranean Sea

FRENCH NORTH AFRICA

PORTUGAL
Lisbon
7th.Aug.1914

In 1912 Serbia, Bulgaria and Greece combined to defeat the Turks, and each gained large slices of territory from Turkey. The enlarged Serbia became a greater threat to Austrian peace and quiet than ever.

Behind Austria stood Germany, who had been her ally since the Dual Alliance had been made by Bismarck in 1879. Bismarck had been successful in keeping German friendship with both Austria and Russia, but when the Kaiser William II took control of policy, the friendship with Russia gave way to suspicion.

RIVAL ALLIANCES

The rivalry between Germany and France was of long standing. In 1870–1, under the leadership of Bismarck, Germany had defeated France and taken from her the provinces of Alsace and Lorraine. It was fear that France would try to get her revenge that had led Bismarck to make the Dual Alliance with Austria. In 1882 he brought Italy into the alliance, which then became the Triple Alliance. This made Germany the strongest power in Europe.

The French certainly wanted their revenge, and they too looked for allies. It was natural that they should turn to Austria's rival, Russia, and in 1892 the Franco-Russian Alliance was formed.

The main continental countries of Europe were thus divided into two fairly even alliances. Italy was a somewhat uncomfortable member of the Triple Alliance, since she wanted to increase her influence in the Balkans, and was not therefore on very good terms with Austria, particularly after Austria's annexation of Bosnia and Herzgovina. At the same time Italy did not wish to see Serbia grow too strong either. Germany encouraged Italy's rivalry with France over colonies in Africa, and so kept her in the alliance for the time being.

THE POSITION OF BRITAIN

Britain in 1900 had no allies, and she began to feel that this was dangerous, especially as there was growing rivalry between her and Germany in commerce and naval building. In 1902 she made an alliance with Japan, and in 1904 she came to a friendly agreement with her old enemy France. This was known as the *Entente Cordiale*.

It was not a definite alliance, in which Britain and France promised to support one another in case of war, but an agreement over colonial questions and a growing friendliness between the two countries.

In 1907 Britain made a friendly agreement with Russia, settling disputes with regard to frontiers in Persia and Afghanistan. The *Entente Cordiale* became the *Triple Entente*, but there were no undertakings to give mutual support in case of war.

Sir Edward Grey, the British Foreign Minister, offered to make a similar friendly agreement with Germany, or any other country. Germany refused, and complained that Britain's real object was to 'encircle the Fatherland'.

Rivalry and suspicion between Britain and Germany increased. Germany had widened the Kiel Canal, so that her warships could get from the Baltic to the North Sea. In 1907 Britain launched the first Dreadnought, by far the most powerful warship yet built. Germany answered by building similar warships. The British government was doubtful about the number of new dreadnoughts she should build, and the speed with which they should be constructed, but there was a great popular outcry for the maximum building programme: 'We want eight, and we won't wait.'

Thus all the major powers had the means to fight an extensive war; popular feeling against possible rivals or enemies was easily whipped up by sections of the press. But in spite of this, many people in Britain believed that the great countries of Europe were too civilized to use their armaments and go to war—they thought that the destructive power of modern armies and navies would make the governments realize that losses would be so heavy that it would not be worth going to war. Few people in Britain thought that, with her little army, Britain would need to enter a war, even if the other countries were foolish enough to fight one another. The British navy was thought of purely as a defensive shield for the British Empire and British trade.

FACTORS TENDING TO UNIFY EUROPE

In some ways Europe was becoming more unified. All countries linked their currencies to the gold standard, so that all were freely interchangeable, and so international trade was made much easier. Foreign travel was simplified and encouraged, and a man could travel without a passport almost anywhere. Industry was becoming more and more international: many firms had foreign branches, and trade agreements sometimes almost ignored national boundaries. International co-operation over such things as postal services

The first Dreadnought

worked smoothly, and increasing numbers of scientists, scholars, sportsmen and others paid visits to, and held conferences in other countries; and yet there was this national rivalry and threat of war.

The leaders of the trade unions, workers' and socialist parties in the leading countries held international conferences, and agreed that they must all take action to prevent their governments from entering on a war which they believed could be of no benefit to the working people anywhere. They discussed the possibility, if a war should start, of nation-wide strikes in all countries concerned, to paralyze the war machine and bring the fighting to a close.

Quarrels and disputes between the nations continued, however; armies and navies were increased, railways that might be useful in war were constructed. There were threats from Germany, conferences were held, France made concessions to Germany, and Europe lurched from one crisis to another.

The British army was modernized by R. B. Haldane, and an expeditionary force was organized, so that it would be ready for immediate service overseas, and there were staff talks between the leaders of the British and French armies, but still no treaty for mutual help in case of war.

The rapid growth of the German navy led the British Admiralty to keep the main British fleet in home waters, and to press for close co-operation with France so that the French navy could concentrate on the Mediterranean, guaranteeing the safety of both British and French interests there, while the British navy would protect the French Atlantic coasts. This was agreed in 1912.

The annexation of Bosnia and Herzgovina, a crisis in connection with French influence in Morocco in 1911, two Balkans wars in 1912 and 1913 were all settled without involving any Great Power in war, and it almost seemed that the optimists were right, and that major war might be avoided after all. 1914 dawned, a year of hope: the spring was unusually peaceful. Sir Edward Grey was doing all he could to come to an agreement with Germany. Britain and Germany had friendly talks on the question of sharing control of the Portuguese colonies in Africa, and they worked together well in helping to settle affairs after the Balkan Wars. Even Russia and Austria seemed to be in agreement. But the rivalries were too bitter, the ambitions of the governments too irreconcilable, the influence of the military leaders too great. One incident was sufficient to set in train the series of decisions which plunged the world into war.

Documentary Two

Europe before 1914

In 1914 Europe was a single civilized community more so even than at the height of the Roman Empire. A man could travel across the length and breadth of the Continent without a passport until he reached the frontiers of Russia and the Ottoman empire. He could settle in a foreign country for work or leisure without legal formalities. . . . Every currency was as good as gold. . . . There were common political forms. . . . Nearly everywhere men could be sure of reasonably fair treatment in the courts of law. No one was killed for religious reasons. No one was killed for political reasons. . . .

From FROM SARAJEVO TO POTSDAM by A. J. P. Taylor (Thames & Hudson)

All the great states of Europe before 1914 were in a condition of aggressive nationalism and drifting towards war; the government of Germany did but lead the general movement. She fell into the pit first, and she floundered deepest. She became the dreadful example at which all her fellow sinners could cry out.

From THE OUTLINE OF HISTORY by H. G. Wells (Cassell)

British and French staff talks

We must be free to go to the help of France as well as free to stand aside. . . . If there were no military plans made beforehand we should be unable to come to the assistance of France in time. . . . We should in effect not have preserved our freedom to help France, but have cut ourselves off from the possibility of doing so.

From TWENTY-FIVE YEARS by Sir Edward Grey (Hodder & Stoughton)

German naval expansion

The Germans had drifted into naval expansion, partly for reasons of domestic politics, partly from a general desire for grandeur. They certainly hoped that a great navy would make the British respect, and even fear, them; they never understood that, unless they could actually outbuild Great Britain, the only effect of this naval competition would be to estrange her.

From THE STRUGGLE FOR MASTERY IN EUROPE 1848–1918 by A. J. P. Taylor (Oxford)

Was Britain committed? Two statements in August 1909

. . . the two great groups of Powers, ourselves, France and Russia on one side and the Triple Alliance on the other.

From BRITISH DOCUMENTS, Minute by Sir Edward Grey, 21st August

Great Britain, owing to her insular position, and having no alliance with any Great Power in Europe, stands alone, and is the pacific advocate of a friendly grouping of the European Powers.

Memorandum by Hardinge, Permanent Under-Secretary, 25th August

Russia and the Straits

On the Bosphorus there can be only the Turks or ourselves.

Sazonov, Russian Foreign Minister, December 1912

. . . the struggle for Constantinople would hardly be possible without a general war . . . unless the active participation of both France and England in joint measures were assured, it does not appear possible to resort to measures of pressure such as might lead to war with Germany.

From a statement by Zhilinski, Russian Chief-of-Staff, January 1914

Austria and Serbia

. . . as soon as our prestige demands, we must intervene in Serbia with vigour, and we could be sure of his (the Kaiser's) support.

Francis Ferdinand, heir to the Austrian throne, November 1912

German ideas on war

Perpetual peace is a dream, and it is not even a beautiful dream. War is an element in the order of the world ordained by God. Without war the world would stagnate and lose itself in materialism.

Count Moltke, Chief of German General Staff under Bismarck

As yet no means are known which call so much into action as a great war, that rough energy born of the camp, that deep impersonality born of hatred, that conscience born of murder and cold-bloodedness, that fervour born of effort in the annihilation of the enemy, that proud indifference to loss, to one's own existence, to that of one's fellows, that earthquake-like soul-shaking which a people needs when it is losing its vitality.

Friedrich Nietzsche, German philosopher, 1844–1900

Germany and Russia

A European war must come sooner or later in which ultimately the struggle will be one between Germanism and Slavism.

Moltke the younger, German General,
in a letter to Conrad, Austro-Hungarian Chief-of-Staff,
February 1913

Russo-Prussian relations are dead once and for all! We have become enemies!

Kaiser William II, February 1914

Working-class action to prevent war

If war threatens to break out it is the duty of the working class in the countries concerned and of their Parliamentary representatives, with the help of the International Socialist Bureau as a means of co-ordinating their action, to use every effort to prevent war by all the means which seem to them most appropriate, having regard to the sharpness of the class war and to the general political situation.

Should war none the less break out, their duty is to intervene to bring it promptly to an end, and with all their energies to use the political and economic crisis created by the war to rouse the populace from its slumbers, and to hasten the fall of capitalist domination.

Resolution passed at the 1907 International Socialist Conference

THE ASSASSINATION AT SARAJEVO

On the 28th June 1914, the Archduke Francis Ferdinand, heir to the throne of Austria–Hungary, was shot in the streets of Sarajevo. The shots were fired by a student from Serbia. There were many Serbians living in Austria, and the Serbian government was always ready to encourage them to revolt. The Austrian government was anxious to weaken Serbia, and thought that this murder would provide a good opportunity: it accused the Serbian government of being responsible for the murder. Germany agreed that this was the time for Austria to destroy the independence of Serbia.

Austria sent an ultimatum (a demand threatening war) to Serbia, so harsh that, had the Serbians accepted it completely, it would have meant practically the end of Serbia as an independent country.

Sir Edward Grey offered to try to arrange an agreement between Serbia and Austria–Hungary, and urged Austria to give Serbia more time to make her reply, but without avail.

The German government advised Austria to declare war on Serbia unless she obtained a satisfactory reply to her ultimatum. The Russians looked upon themselves as Serbia's protectors, but the Kaiser believed that they were not ready for war. He hoped that a threat from Germany would be sufficient to prevent Russia from coming to the aid of Serbia.

Sir Edward Grey sent urgent invitations to the ambassadors of the powers to attend a conference, and begged them not to start a war until after it had met, but Germany rejected the idea of a conference.

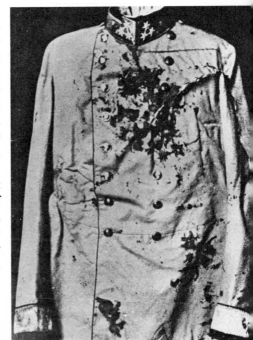

Archduke Francis Ferdinand's tunic

Students and young workers volunteer for the German army

Serbia sent her reply on 25th July. She gave in on so many points that, when the Kaiser saw it, he said, 'It is a great moral success for Austria; but with it all reason for war is gone.' But·it was too late: Austria was determined on war, and saying that the reply was not satisfactory, she declared war on Serbia on 28th July. The First World War had begun.

The vital question now was, what would Russia do? Sir Edward Grey begged Germany to try, by any method she could, to prevent war between Austria and Russia. But again it was too late—Russia had already begun to mobilize her forces to come to the aid of Serbia. Messages passed between the Kaiser and the Tsar, but they were now helpless—the army leaders were in control, and they thought the time for war had come.

The next step would be mobilization by Germany against Russia. Grey warned Germany that if the war spread to the other great powers, Britain might have to come in on the side of France. The Kaiser was very angry, and called the English low-down, shop-keeping knaves, and Grey a contemptible scoundrel. There had just been giant strikes in England, and trouble in Ireland; to many people Britain seemed to be on the brink of revolution and civil war. The Kaiser had been confident that Britain would not enter the war, but he was not really worried, for the German generals were quite prepared for British entry and had allowed for this in their plan. They did not expect Britain to be able to play an important part in the war if she did come in, for Germany had a plan by which she expected to beat France very quickly, and after the defeat of France, Britain, with her tiny army, would be helpless.

THE SCHLIEFFEN PLAN

For many years Germany had feared a war on two fronts, that is, a war against France in the west and Russia in the east at the same time. A German general named Schlieffen had worked out a plan. It was expected that the Russians would take a long time to get their large armies into action, so the Germans hoped to defeat France in a lightning campaign of a few weeks. They could then turn all their forces against Russia.

The frontier between France and Germany was very well guarded with strong lines of fortifications, but that between France and Belgium was not strongly fortified. The Germans therefore intended to march most of their army through Belgium, and enter France across the weakly defended Belgian frontier. Their main forces would then pass north and west of Paris, take the city in the rear, and encircle the French armies. In such a short war Britain's navy could do nothing, and all would be over before she could bring an army of any size into the field (see map on p. 31).

With Britain thus written off, Germany could support her ally Austria against Russia, even if it did mean fighting France as well and war on two fronts. She warned Russia that if her mobilization did not stop at once Germany would mobilize too, in defence of Austria. On 1st August she declared war on Russia.

THE POSSIBILITY OF NEUTRALITY

The war was no longer a question of an Austrian attack upon Serbia —it had now become a clash of the Great Powers and their alliances, a struggle for mastery. Germany asked France for a promise that she would remain neutral in a war between Germany and Russia. She replied: 'France will act in accordance with her interests.'

France could not afford to see Russia, her only firm ally, beaten by Austria and Germany, and she began to mobilize her forces. She was, however, even more anxious than Germany to know what Britain would do.

Most people in Britain, most Members of Parliament, were quite certain that Britain should keep out of the war, but Sir Edward Grey knew that her naval agreement with France would make it impossible for her to stand aside. Although it was possible that the Germans would have agreed not to attack France in the Channel, in order to secure Britain's neutrality, Grey felt that the spirit of the agreement required that Britain should give France positive support. He also feared that if Germany were allowed to crush France, she would later turn upon Britain. Germany would then be stronger than ever, and Britain might have no allies.

Grey knew that if he suggested entering the war at once, most of the Members of Parliament would vote against him, and the whole country would be bitterly divided. So when the French Ambassador asked him whether Britain would at least give the French the support of her navy, Grey could not promise. The Ambassador went out, pale and desperate. 'They are going to betray us, they are going to betray us,' he said.

Like Germany, however, France did not allow doubts about the possible neutrality of Britain to lead to any hesitation in entering the war, and she continued to mobilize. Like the German generals, the French generals also had a plan, which they believed would enable them to defeat the Germans.

On 2nd August the German Ambassador saw Mr. Asquith, the British Prime Minister, and, with tears in his eyes, begged him not to support France. 'A war between our two countries is unthinkable,' said Mr. Asquith. His words may be taken at their face value since, only a week before, half of the Cabinet had threatened to resign if Britain declared war. On the other hand, extensive preparations had been made and heads of the armed forces both in Britain and in the Empire had already been alerted. Asquith may also have been alluding to the fact that the Kaiser and King George V were second cousins through Queen Victoria.

Again the French Ambassador asked Grey whether Britain would stand by her ally, and again Grey could not say that she would. In an interview that evening with Wickham Steed, the Political Director of *The Times*, he said: 'I wonder whether we should not, this very evening, cross out the word *honour* from the English vocabulary.' But at that very moment German forces were putting the Schlieffen Plan into operation, marching through Luxembourg, and massing on the frontier of Belgium. The Germans were about to make sure

that the British Parliament and people would be almost completely
united in entering the war.

THE INVASION OF BELGIUM

All the Great Powers, including Germany and Britain, had promised
the little country of Belgium that none of them would ever attack
her, but that they would come to her defence if she were attacked.
On 2nd August the Germans demanded the peaceful passage of
German troops through Belgium. The Belgians refused, and on 3rd
August the Germans began an invasion of Belgium with large forces.

The British may not have had a definite treaty obligation to go to
the help of France, but they had with Belgium. Sir Edward Grey

BRAVO, BELGIUM!

How 'Punch' saw the invasion of Belgium

made a long speech in the House of Commons as soon as the news of the German invasion of Belgium came through. He gave his reasons why Britain should enter the war, and carried almost the whole House with him. Afterwards, when he was congratulated on his speech, he crashed his fist on the table, crying 'I hate war! I hate war!' As he stood that evening watching, from the windows of the Foreign Office, the lights winking in the dusk, he said to a friend: 'The lamps are going out all over Europe; we shall not see them lit again in our lifetime.'

An ultimatum was sent to Germany, warning that if the Germans did not withdraw their forces from Belgium by midnight, Britain would be at war with Germany. No reply was received and at 11 p.m. London time, midnight in Berlin, 4th August 1914, Britain entered the war.

Waiting to hear news outside the Houses of Parliament, 4th August, 1914

A few days previously Britain had seemed completely divided and distracted by strikes, suffragette violence and threats of civil war in northern Ireland. During the first three days of August there had been great protest meetings against the war, and Neutrality Committees had been set up, supported by Labour leaders, scholars such as Sir Gilbert Murray, Oxford and Cambridge professors, prominent Liberals and others. The Cabinet itself had been divided; but after the German invasion of Belgium a great change took place, and almost all opposition to the war melted away. Only John Burns and John Morley in the Government still stood for neutrality. The Labour Party and the trade unions swung over to support for the war. Ramsay MacDonald, the Chairman of the Parliamentary Labour Party, who with two or three other socialists opposed the war, was forced to resign.

As soon as they heard of the invasion of Belgium and of Britain's entry into the war, huge cheering crowds gathered in the streets. Thousands thronged the recruiting offices, eager to join the army. Suddenly almost the whole country was united and full of vigour and determination.

WAR AIMS

Most of the British people entered the war feeling that they were fighting in a good cause: they were fighting to defend Belgium, they were fighting to defend freedom and democracy (although their ally Russia was one of the least democratic countries in the world), they were fighting to put an end to the German militarism, the power of the German army to override the freedom of other peoples. They hoped that it would be a war to end war, that once they had won the war there would never be the need for war, and that it would be a better world, which would be safe for small countries, safe for ordinary people everywhere.

In other countries, on both sides in the war, the same enthusiastic crowds welcomed it, all believing that right was on their side, and that they were fighting for security and freedom.

Although the Germans were prepared to risk Britain's entry into the war, they certainly did not realize how immediate and how widespread would be the response of the British people to the invasion of Belgium. The Germans thought of a treaty as something to be broken if it suited them. Bethmann–Hollweg, the German Chancellor, justified the invasion of Belgium in the name of 'necessity' and angrily told the British Ambassador in Berlin that Britain was entering the war merely for a 'scrap of paper', and that Britain would be responsible for all the horror that would follow.

What the German Chancellor called a 'scrap of paper': the Treaty of London (1839) by which Britain, Austria, France, Prussia (Germany) and Russia guaranteed Belgian independence from Holland. The last page shows the seals of all these countries and the signatures of their Foreign Ministers (Britain and Belgium head the list).

même tems, les ordres nécessaires pour la remise de ces territoires,
villes, places, et lieux, aux Commissaires qui seront désignés à
cet effet de part et d'autre.–

   Cette évacuation et cette remise s'effectueront de
manière à pouvoir être terminées dans l'espace de quinze
jours, ou plutôt si faire se peut.–

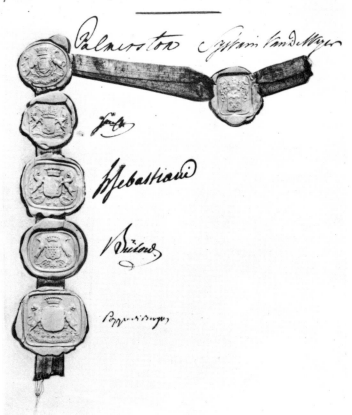

Documentary Three

Declaring war

Those who urged a clear British line did so from contradictory motives. Nicolson (British diplomatist) feared that Russia and France would win a complete victory and that the British Empire would then be at their mercy. Eyre Crowe (British diplomatist), more representative of official opinion, feared that France would be defeated and that Great Britain would then be at the mercy of Germany. In any case it was impossible for Grey to make any clear declaration; public opinion would not have allowed it. If there is a criticism of Grey, it must be that he had not educated the British public enough in the previous years. No doubt he had shrunk from increasing the tension in Europe.

From THE STRUGGLE FOR MASTERY IN EUROPE 1848–1918
by A. J. P. Taylor (Oxford)

The Cabinet, July 1914

Our relations (those of Britain and Germany) are very much better than they were a few years ago. . . . The two great Empires begin to realize they can co-operate for common ends, and that the points of co-operation are greater and more numerous and more important than the points of possible controversy.

HANSARD, fifth series, LXV 727, 23rd July 1914,
speech by Lloyd George

There could be no question of our taking part in any war in the first instance. He (Lloyd George) knew of no Minister who would be in favour of it.

From C. P. SCOTT OF THE MANCHESTER GUARDIAN by J. L. Hammond (Bell)
quoting Memorandum by Scott, 27th July 1914

A poet's reaction

FIVE SOULS

First Soul

I was a peasant of the Polish plain ;
I left my plough because the message ran :
Russia in danger, needed every man
To save her from the Teuton ; and was slain.
I gave my life for freedom—This I know :
For those who bade me fight had told me so.

Second Soul

I was a Tyrolese, a mountaineer ;
I gladly left my mountain home to fight
Against the brutal treacherous Muscovite ;
And died in Poland on a Cossack spear.
I gave my life for freedom—This I know :
For those who bade me fight had told me so.

Third Soul

> *I worked in Lyons at my weaver's loom,*
> *When suddenly the Prussian despot hurled*
> *His felon blow at France and at the world ;*
> *Then I went forth to Belgium and my doom.*
> *I gave my life for freedom—This I know :*
> *For those who bade me fight had told me so.*

Fourth Soul

> *I owned a vineyard by the wooded Main,*
> *Until the Fatherland, begirt by foes*
> *Lusting her downfall, called me, and I rose*
> *Swift to the call—and died in far Lorraine.*
> *I gave my life for freedom—This I know :*
> *For those who bade me fight had told me so.*

Fifth Soul

> *I worked in a great shipyard by the Clyde ;*
> *Then came a sudden word of wars declared,*
> *Of Belgium, peaceful, helpless, unprepared,*
> *Asking our aid : I joined the ranks, and died.*
> *I gave my life for freedom—This I know :*
> *For those who bade me fight had told me so.*

W. N. Ewer

From POEMS OF REVOLT (Noel Douglas)

A pacifist's verdict

Great Britain had, by a solemn treaty more than once renewed, pledged herself to maintain the neutrality of Belgium. . . . Germany suddenly and without excuse invaded Belgium. . . . Our answer was : 'Evacuate Belgium within twelve hours or we fight you.'

I think that answer was right . . . I feel that in this case I would rather die than submit ; and I believe that the Government, in deciding to keep its word at the cost of war, has rightly interpreted the feelings of the average British citizen.

From HOW CAN WAR EVER BE RIGHT?
by Professor Gilbert Murray (Allen & Unwin)

Austria–Hungary's ultimatum to Serbia

It was an ultimatum such as had never been penned in modern times . . . it seemed absolutely impossible that any state in the world could accept it, or that any acceptance, however abject, would satisfy the aggressor.

From THE WORLD CRISIS by Winston Churchill (Odhams)
First Lord of the Admiralty

Mobilization

The (French) Cabinet met at 9 a.m. General Joffre repeated the explanations which he had given me, concerning the necessity to mobilize. No objection was raised, no comment made. The ministers all agreed that we should face essential obligations at once, but they also insisted that, to the very last minute, no effort to preserve peace should be spared.

I shall never forget that supreme moment when I released the order. . . . Within three hours its contents were known throughout all of France. There was not a single village or hamlet . . . which did not receive the stunning news. And the whole French nation arose at once, ready for war.

Raymond Recouly, journalist,
reporting the words of Adolphe Messimy, French Secretary of War,
in LES HEURES TRAGIQUES D'AVANT-GUERRE

The electric spark of the Mobilization Decree, on August 1st 1914, fired a train of indescribable enthusiasm from Memel to the tiniest hamlet in the southern German mountains, enthusiasm which in its volume and unity swept everything irresistibly before it. Everyone, whether soldier or civilian, man or woman, realised the right was on our side and wanted to share the duty and responsibility of the common defence of our sorely-menaced Fatherland. . . . The oppressive ring of 'encirclement' was at last to be broken.

From MY WAR EXPERIENCES by Crown Prince William of Germany
(Hurst & Blackett)

After the final prayer the court chaplain read the Tsar's manifesto to his people—a simple recital of the events which have made war inevitable, an eloquent appeal to all the national energies, an invocation to the Most High, and so forth. Then the Tsar went up to the altar and raised his right hand toward the gospel held out to him. . . . In a slow, low voice he made the following declaration :

'Officers of my guard, here present, I greet in you my whole army and give it my blessing. I solemnly swear that I will never make peace so long as one of the enemy is on the soil of the fatherland.' A wild outburst of cheering was the answer to this declaration. For nearly ten minutes there was a frantic tumult in the gallery, and it was soon intensified by the cheers of the crowd massed along the Neva.

The Emperor appeared on the balcony. The entire crowd at once knelt and sang the Russian national anthem.

From AN AMBASSADOR'S MEMOIRS by Maurice Paléologue (Hutchinson)

On the morning of the 30th (July), Nicholas wired the Kaiser an explanation of Russia's partial mobilization :

'The military measures which have now come into force were decided five days ago for reasons of defence on account of Austria's preparations. I hope with all my heart that these measures won't interfere with your part as mediator which I greatly value. We need your strong pressure on Austria to come to an understanding with us. Nicky'.

. . . Before news of Russia's general mobilization reached Berlin, two more

telegrams passed between Potsdam and Tsarkoe Selo (the Tsar's residence). First, Nicholas cabled to the Kaiser: 'It is technically impossible for me to suspend my military preparations. But as long as conversations with Austria are not broken off, my troops will refrain from taking the offensive anyway. I give you my word of honour on that. Nicky'.

William replied:
'I have gone to the utmost limits possible in my efforts to save peace. It is not I who will bear the responsibility for the terrible disaster which now threatens the civilized world. You and you alone can still avert it. My friendship for you and your empire which my grandfather bequeathed to me on his deathbed is still sacred to me and I have been loyal to Russia when she was in trouble, notably during your last war. Even now, you can still save the peace of Europe by stopping your military measures. Willy'.

News of the general mobilization of the huge Russian army caused consternation in Berlin. At midnight on July 31, Count Pourtalés (the German ambassador) appeared in Sazanov's office with a German ultimatum to Russia to halt the mobilization within twelve hours. At noon the following day, August 1, Russia had not replied, and the Kaiser ordered general mobilization.

Nicholas hurriedly telegraphed to William:
'I understand that you are compelled to mobilize but I should like to have the same guarantee from you that I gave you myself—that these measures do not mean war and that we shall continue to negotiate to save the general peace so dear to our hearts. With God's help our long and tried friendship should be able to prevent bloodshed. I confidently await your reply. Nicky'.

Before this message arrived in Berlin, however, coded instructions had been sent by the German government to Count Pourtalés in St. Petersburg. He was instructed to declare war on Russia at 5 p.m. . . . .

Quoted in NICHOLAS AND ALEXANDRA by Robert K. Massie (Gollancz)

George V's appeal to the Tsar

After dinner on Friday he (Asquith) was sitting in Downing Street with Grey and Churchill when Sir William Tyrrell arrived from the Foreign Office with a message from the embassy in Berlin suggesting that if Russian mobilization could be held up, the Kaiser might be willing to restrain Austria: 'We all set to work . . . to draft a direct personal appeal from the King to the Tsar, and when it was settled I called a taxi and . . . drove to Buckingham Palace at about 1.30 a.m. The poor King was hauled out of bed and one of my strangest experiences . . . was sitting with him—he in a brown dressing-gown over his nightshirt and with copious signs of having been aroused from his first "beauty sleep"—while I read the message and the proposed answer. All he did was to suggest that it should be more personal and direct—by the insertion of the words "My dear Nicky" and the addition at the end of the signature "Georgie".'

From ASQUITH by Roy Jenkins (Collins)

THE INVASION OF FRANCE

When Britain declared war on Germany, the German forces were already advancing through Luxembourg and Belgium, ready to launch their all-out attack on France. The British Government agreed that the whole British Expeditionary Force of 90,000 men in England should be moved to northern France as quickly and secretly as possible. The Germans had nothing but contempt for the little British army, and they did nothing to prevent its crossing which was closely covered by the navy. Not a single ship was sunk, not a man drowned.

'We'll be back by Christmas,' cried the troops cheerfully, as they embarked. Nearly everyone expected it to be a short war—the trained professional British army, with the help of the French, would soon finish off the German conscript men. Meanwhile the British navy would protect the home country, and life could go on in normal fashion. 'Business as usual' was the motto. 'Business as usual' said the notices in the shop windows, 'Take your holidays as usual' said the posters of the London Brighton and South Coast Railway.

Bayonet practice in spurs—how they thought the war would be won

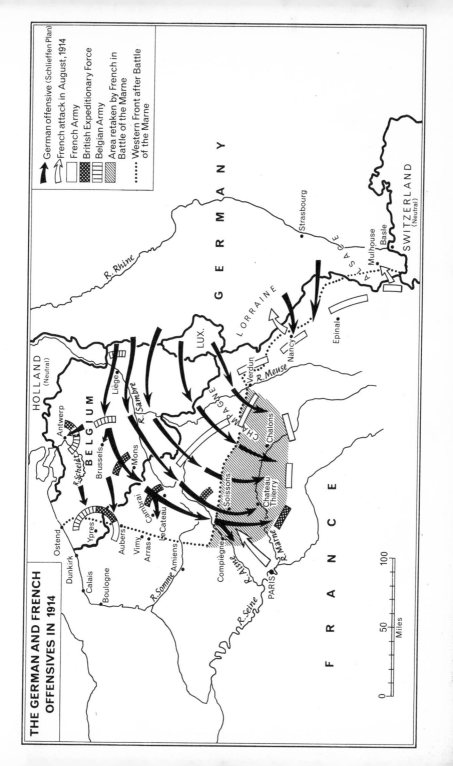

THE GERMAN AND FRENCH OFFENSIVES IN 1914

German offensive (Schlieffen Plan)
French attack in August, 1914
French Army
British Expeditionary Force
Belgian Army
Area retaken by French in Battle of the Marne
Western Front after Battle of the Marne

GERMANY

HOLLAND (Neutral)

SWITZERLAND (Neutral)

FRANCE

BELGIUM

LUX.

ALSACE

LORRAINE

CHAMPAGNE

R. Rhine

R. Scheldt

R. Sambre

R. Meuse

R. Somme

R. Aisne

R. Seine

R. Marne

Antwerp
Ostend
Dunkirk
Calais
Boulogne
Ypres
Aubers
Vimy
Arras
Amiens
Cambrai
Le Cateau
Mons
Brussels
Liège
Compiègne
Soissons
Château Thierry
PARIS
Chalons
Verdun
Nancy
Epinal
Strasbourg
Mulhouse
Basle

0   50   100
Miles

A Belgian soldier trying to keep out the Germans and the cold

In France and Belgium it was a very different story. There the Germans were putting the Schlieffen Plan into operation. Nothing was so important to the Germans as the Schlieffen Plan, which was to win the war for them. By its use they would beat the French, then they would beat the Russians; Britain could be dealt with later.

Seven-eighths of the German troops were massed for the invasion of France, most of them on the right of the German line, to go through Belgium. Only a small holding force of Germans was retained on the Russian frontier to meet the expected Russian attack in the east. If the Russians overran East Prussia, that must be borne; if the French successfully invaded Alsace and Lorraine, that too must be put up with; if the advance through Belgium brought Britain into the war, that also would not be too high a price to pay for the Schlieffen Plan which was to win the war for Germany.

General Schlieffen was dead, but his plan was to be carried out exactly as he had laid it down; so two million men massed for the invasion of France. The Belgians and French expected that the great fortresses, particularly that at Namur, would hold up the German advance for a long time, but the Germans had prepared for this. They had constructed far heavier guns than had ever been used before in land fighting and they could bombard forts whilst out of range of the defending guns. This was the first of the German surprises in the war. The forts were shattered by the massive artillery fire, and the Germans swept on.

The French had a plan which they thought would foil the Germans. The right wing of their army was to attack in force and advance north-eastwards, cutting off the German armies from their supplies. The French soldiers went into the attack in bright, colourful uniforms, cheering, and their bands playing the *Marseillaise*. They formed a perfect target for the German gunners, and were mown down by machine-gun and rifle fire. Three hundred thousand Frenchmen were killed, wounded or taken prisoner. The French hopes of a general advance withered away as the Germans poured across northern France.

MONS

The British army, under the command of Sir John French, moved up to the little Belgian town of Mons, marching along the hot, dusty roads. At the line of the Mons-Conde Canal they came in touch with the German First Army under von Kluck, the army whose part in the Schlieffen Plan was to move rapidly south-west and pass to the west of Paris.

At Mons there were six German divisions facing two British. The Germans advanced, marching in mass down the road, singing their marching songs. The British had taken hasty cover, and were waiting.

'Now, from their rough trenches along the canal bank, from the houses, from the slopes of the slag-heaps, they opened the aimed rapid rifle fire which was the old Army's pride. The Germans came on as bravely as ever, but the rifle fire scythed into the solid blocks of them and the blocks vanished. At that range the bullets' trajectory was flat, and in that formation each bullet went through two or three men before spending its force. Grey corpses piled up along the canal bank and in the grubby fields.'★

So rapid and deadly was the rifle fire that the Germans thought the British must be armed with machine guns.

More and more Germans entered the battle, and by late afternoon it was clear that they were too strong to be held any longer, and the order was given to withdraw. The retreat from Mons had begun.

Almost surrounded, they were forced to retreat along the roads by which they had just come. Weary and footsore, and under constant German fire, they slowly gave ground.

★ *From Fourteen Eighteen* by John Masters (Joseph), p. 15.

French refugees

The roads were now crowded. As the British retreated, the country people moved with them—there was no 'Business as Usual' for them. At every farm and cottage, carts and wagons were being loaded with furniture, spare clothing, food, everything moveable, with children and old people perched on the top. For mile after mile, an endless line of handcarts, dog carts, ox wagons, bicycles and barrows, all loaded with household goods, wound slowly along the roads to the south and west.

The noise of the guns grew louder, and now and then a shell, bursting in a cloud of dense black smoke, would spread terror and death. To the soldiers guns were more important than people—the Germans must not be allowed to capture the guns—so the refugees were forced off the roads into the fields to make way, and the guns lumbered on.

The Germans followed closely. Then at Le Cateau the British turned. Though they had not eaten or slept, they held up the German advance for twenty-four hours. Then the retreat continued. Often marching for most of the night and fighting most of the day, they moved southwards and westwards, back and back, until the sign posts said *Paris 44 km* (27 miles). 'Next stop the Pyrenees,' they said, their habitual cheerfulness hiding a growing and secret dismay. They had reached the river Marne.

THE EASTERN FRONT

The news in Britain was confused, and the air was full of rumours. Huge German losses were reported, and enormous French victories. The people were warned not to believe these reports, and it soon became clear that things were not going so well—the British and French were being forced to retreat. But there were the Russians. The 'Russian steamroller' would crush its way into Berlin. Not only that, the Russians were coming to the help of the West. Stories were told of fur-hatted Russian troops on the quay at Leith, of ghostly trains passing southwards through the Midlands, the windows filled with bearded Russian faces. There was no doubt who they were—in this hot August weather someone had seen them stamping the snow off their boots. But these were baseless rumours: in the wartime state of fear and excitement, people seemed ready to believe anything. There was not a Russian soldier in Britain or France. They were all in the east, marching to their doom in East Prussia.

The Russians had moved more quickly than the Germans had expected, and they were already advancing far into eastern Germany. The Schlieffen Plan appeared to be working so well, however, that Moltke, the Commander-in-Chief, felt that he could spare some of his troops to meet the Russian menace, and soon thirty-two train-loads of German troops were making the seven-hundred-mile journey across Germany, moving from the Western Front. By the time they arrived, the danger was over—the Russians had been utterly defeated at the battle of Tannenberg.

The Russians under General Samsonov had advanced into East Prussia and defeated and driven back the Prussians at Gumbinnen,

General Ludendorff, second-in-command to Hindenburg and mastermind of the first major German victory, at Lake Tannenberg

but their main forces were concentrated against the Austrians at Lemberg.

Von Hindenburg concentrated all the German troops in the east in an attack on Samsonov's army, and by a skilful enveloping movement, confined most of the Russian troops in swampy country where they were pounded by a ring of heavy guns. Thousands of Russians were driven into the lakes and morasses of Tannenberg and machine-gunned as they struggled in the mud and water.

The troops from the Western Front who arrived a few days later were no longer needed to defend East Prussia, but they were too late to prevent the utter defeat of the Austrians by another Russian army at Lemberg. Slav officers in the Austrian army had revealed their strategy to the Russians who, by this victory, overran Galicia, the north-eastern corner of the Austrian empire. Austrian prisoners and casualties totalled 130,000.

No news of the disaster of Tannenberg was allowed to reach the British people for a long time, and people in Britain still spoke hopefully of immense Russian military strength.

It was impossible, however, to keep all the bad news from the people in Britain, and anxiety grew. Large wall maps were issued by the daily papers, and in thousands of homes the positions of the armies were shown by lines of little flags, and day after day the flags were moved back, as the retreat went on.

THE BATTLE OF THE MARNE

The German advance in France continued for several days, but the first hints of anxiety began to trouble the German commanders. Where were the masses of prisoners and captured guns that should have been taken from a routed enemy? Were the French and British really so badly beaten? The advancing German troops also became less confident. Even German organizational skill was not equal to the task of moving such vast numbers of men and quantities of supplies in strict accordance with the Plan.

The German First and Second Armies which should have swung round to the west of Paris found themselves out of touch with the German troops on their left. There were now not enough troops to keep a continuous front and also to carry out the plan to encircle Paris; nor was there the heavy artillery to carry out a frontal attack on the city. Some of the needed troops were seven hundred miles away in East Prussia, and others had been moved eastwards to meet the French attempt at invasion in Alsace. The artillery was held up at the siege of the great Belgian port and fortress of Antwerp. So the German First and Second Armies turned south and then south-east, leaving Paris to the west (see map on p. 31.).

They crossed the river Marne, the British still retreating before them, but as they passed Paris, they left their flank open. The French Sixth Army was stationed for the defence of the capital, and as the tide of battle swept to the east of the city, General Galliéni, the Governor of Paris, urged its commander, General Manoury, to leave the city and attack von Kluck's right and rear. Using every possible taxi and bus, they rushed into the attack. The German First Army was forced to wheel round to face this challenge from the west and north-west. Their supply lines were being threatened, so they recrossed the Marne and retired northwards.

The German Second Army then found that its flank had also become exposed, and it too swung round, but too late to prevent the formation of a gap of thirty miles between itself and the First Army.

General Joffre, Commander-in-Chief of the French armies, decided that now was the time for a counter attack, and on 4th September he put out his Order of the Day Number 6, ordering the Allied armies to turn about and face the enemy. He telegraphed to the Ministry of War in Paris: 'The struggle which is about to take place may have decisive results. It may also, in the case of a reverse, have the gravest consequences for the country.'

On 5th September the Battle of the Marne began. It was described by Winston Churchill as the greatest battle that was ever fought in the history of the world. It was certainly a turning point in the war.

With General Joffre's order, the long retreat of the British army was over at last. The way was open for a rapid cavalry advance northwards into the gap between the German First and Second Armies, an advance which might have broken the First Army's lines of communication and brought them to disaster, but Sir John French did not wish to run the risk of being crushed between the two German armies, and did not move too quickly.

The French were now attacking all along the line, and so grave did the danger appear to the German Commander-in-Chief that he ordered a general withdrawal, and the Germans retreated to the line of the Aisne. The Battle of the Marne, the most important in the whole war, was over. The German generals had failed to carry out the Schlieffen Plan, and the whole campaign, with its objective of quick and complete victory, had failed. Paris was saved, the French armies were saved, the whole Allied cause was saved. For the first time the little flags on the maps at home were moved forwards, and hope revived.

General Joffre, Commander-in-Chief of the French army until 1916

YPRES

When they reached the Aisne, the Germans stood firm. Then both sides began a race to the north, each side trying to outflank the other. The Germans now realized the value of the British army and of British supplies to the Allied armies in France, and they hoped to gain control of the Channel ports, and so cut off easy communications with England. To the Allies it was vitally important to prevent this.

The Belgians had been stubbornly defending Antwerp, but the German pressure increased, and the Belgian army was faced with the threat of being cut off from their allies. They therefore withdrew on 9th October, and linked up with the British and French troops, leaving the deserted city to the Germans. They hindered a German advance along the coast to Ostend by flooding the *polders*.

Meanwhile the British had moved northwards from the Aisne into western Belgium, and with French and Belgian troops, completed the Allied line to the coast. They were contemplating a great attack which would drive the Germans back to the river Scheldt, when the Germans began a powerful offensive towards Ypres and the Yser river. The German headquarters issued the famous order of the day: 'The German forces will march over Sir John French and his contemptible little army.'

A complete German breakthrough here would have faced the British army with the alternatives of surrender or being driven into the sea. They therefore held on grimly until relief arrived. Sir John French quickly concentrated his forces in this vital area, and General Joffre sent French troops to his aid, while at the same time meeting other German attacks further south.

On 27th October, the Germans began an even fiercer assault, in an attempt to break through at Ypres. The British were forced back, but by nightfall the lost ground was recovered. There were no great strategic moves in this battle of Ypres, but just savage frontal attacks and stubborn resistance and counter attacks. Every village, every house, every tree was used as cover, and for weeks the desperate struggle went on until there was nothing left but smouldering ruins and shattered stumps of trees. Across the desolate waste wandered thousands of starving Belgian refugees, glad to devour the rotting carcasses of horses and cattle which lay in ditches and shell holes.

In another great attack on 1st November, the Germans again advanced, but with French help they were checked. On 11th November the Kaiser ordered the famous Prussian Guard to carry the Ypres salient at all costs. They pierced the line but did not break it, and day after day the desperate fighting continued.

Towards the end of November the fighting died down. Rain, floods, mud and appalling losses forced the Germans to realize that their hopes of a real breakthrough were futile. Again the Germans had failed to win the great victory which might have changed the whole course of the war in their favour. The British had suffered terribly heavy losses, but the Allied line, which had reached the sea between Ostend and Dunkirk, retained control of the Channel Ports of Boulogne, Calais and Dunkirk, through which passed increasing numbers of men and quantities of supplies as the British built up a great army in France.

Documentary Four

Brussels on 2nd August

He (the Belgian Vice-Consul in Cologne) was showing signs of great emotion. 'Since six o'clock this morning,' he stated, 'military trains are leaving the Cologne station at the rate of one every three or four minutes. They are not going southeast, en route to France, but in the direction of Aix-la-Chapelle, that is toward Belgium!'

In Brussels, meanwhile, all was quiet. Peaceful crowds dressed in their Sunday best were filling the streets, squares and cafés. No one among the many promenaders foresaw the things to come. Everybody believed in the sanctity of treaties. . . . On that day . . . the German Ambassador once more vouched for his country's friendly intent toward Belgium. 'Perhaps your neighbour's roof will burn,' he stated, 'but your own house will be spared.'

From LES HEURES TRAGIQUES D'AVANT-GUERRE
by Raymond Recouly

The German entry into Brussels

The streets were crowded but hardly a sound was heard, and the Germans took possession of Brussels in silence.

When the Germans entered Brussels the intrepid Burgomaster Max rode at the head of the ill-omened procession, to prove that he was still master in his own house. When the German General ordered three hundred beds to be got ready in the Town Hall, 'See that there are beds in the Town Hall for three hundred and one,' said the Burgomaster, determined not to leave his guests.

Amongst the Brussels women it was etiquette to ignore the German officers. The women would turn their eyes away or even turn their backs upon the officers, thus hurting their arrogant self-esteem.

Burgomaster Max . . . resolutely countered the lying proclamations that were posted upon the walls of Brussels by delivering speeches in the public square, until at length the German Military Governor wrote: 'I have found myself obliged to suspend Burgomaster Max from his office. . . . He is now in honourable custody in a fortress.'

From LIONS LED BY DONKEYS by P. A. Thompson (Werner Laurie)

The British Expeditionary Force—two German views

It is my Royal and Imperial command that you concentrate your energies, for the immediate present, upon one single purpose, and that is that you address all your skill and all the valour of my soldiers to exterminate first the treacherous English, and walk over General French's contemptible little army.

Command from Kaiser William II to von Kluck

I always had the greatest admiration for the British Expeditionary Force. It was the wonderful kernel of a great army. . . . The way the retreat was carried out was remarkable. I tried very hard to outflank them, but I could not do so. If I had succeeded the War would have been won.

General von Kluck, quoted in MEMORIES OF FORTY-EIGHT YEARS' SERVICE, by General Horace Smith-Dorien (Murray)

Paris

August 30th was an unhappy day. In the morning I was received by Monsieur Millerand, Secretary for War, who told me that the military situation was worsening and that the Germans were rapidly nearing the city. I telephoned General Joffre and insisted on the necessity of creating an army strong enough to defend the city outside of its unfinished defence works. . . . I had the impression that he had already given up the defence of Paris, and that he had no intention of depriving his retreating armies of any of their units.

. . . The batteries had no ammunition, the breastworks were hardly begun, the food and supply organization was insufficient. . . .

From MEMOIRES DE GENERAL GALLIÉNI (Payot)

The Battle of the Marne

Then without hurry or emphasis, Joffre explained the situation, developing the story of the German advance, and the change of direction of the German First Army. Here he interrupted his narrative to say that the British Flying Corps had played a prominent, in fact a vital, part in watching and following this all-important movement on which so much depended. Thanks to our aviators, he had been kept accurately and constantly informed of von Kluck's movements. To them he owed the certainty which had enabled him to make his plans in good time.

. . . He was now developing his plan. We hung on his every word. We saw as he evoked it the immense battlefield over which the corps, drawn by the magnet of his will, were moving like pieces of intricate machinery, until they clicked into their appointed places. . . . Joffre seemed to be pointing the Germans out to us—blundering blindly on, hastening to their fate, their huge, massive, dusty columns rushing towards the precipice over which they would soon be rolling.

Joffre was now foretelling what would happen on the morrow, and on the day after, and on the day after that, and as a prophet he was heard with absolute faith.

Joffre was now talking of the British. Again he thanked Sir John for his decision. His plan depended entirely upon British co-operation, its success on their action. . . . Everything the British could give, all they had, was asked for.

. . . We all looked at Sir John. He had understood and was under the stress of strong emotion. Tears stood in his eyes, welled over and rolled down his cheeks.

He tried to say something in French . . . then he exclaimed : 'Damn it, I can't explain. Tell him that all that men can do, our fellows will do.'

From LIAISON 1914 by Brigadier-General E. L. Spears
(Eyre & Spottiswood)

The importance of the Channel ports

'Whatever we achieve against Russia is not an embarrassment but a relief to England. Conditions have forced us to fight on a front which is not in accordance with our political interest. The Russo-German War is very popular in England. The English statesmen are absolutely determined to hold out to the end. We can only save our future by pressure on England. The decision of the war turns exclusively on whether Germany or England can hold out the longer. It is absolutely necessary to occupy Calais and Boulogne.'

This point of view seemed unintelligible to the Chancellor. . . . He failed to realize that England, now that it had once come into the war, was clearly, coolly, and consistently bent on winning it.

From MY MEMOIRS by Grand Admiral von Tirpitz (Hutchinson)

RE-ASSESSMENT

When the opposing armies reached the sea, the second phase of the fighting on the Western Front and the war of movement came to an end. All the governments on both sides had expected the war to be a short one, but now all hopes of winning the war quickly had faded. The French attempt at the invasion of Germany through Alsace and Lorraine had petered out within three weeks, and within five weeks the Germans had to admit that their plan to knock out France had failed. The Russians were farther from Berlin than at the beginning of the war, and Hindenburg's plan to concentrate German and Austrian forces in a combined attack on the Russians in an attempt to defeat her completely, and make her withdraw from the war before the winter, was not put into operation. Hindenburg had appealed to the High Command for large numbers of troops to be transferred from the Western Front, but they were needed in the drive for the Channel Ports; so the fighting on the Eastern Front was mainly indecisive.

Even the Austrian hopes of crushing little Serbia, and making a triumphal entry into Belgrade had come to nothing, as the Serbs fought back strongly, and pushed the Austrians back over the frontier and invaded southern Hungary.

At sea, too, there had been no great victory. The British Navy had not sunk the German High Seas Fleet—it had not been given the chance. Most of the German High Seas Fleet were trapped in harbour as British cruisers maintained the blockade in the North Sea (see map on p. 67). But a few German warships, particularly the *Emden*, did great harm to British shipping in the early years of the war.

Both sides had therefore to reconcile themselves to a long war, and they had to consider the conservation of their resources of manpower and materials. The losses in the three months of open fighting had been terribly heavy: the French had lost 854,000 men killed, wounded and prisoners, the British 85,000 and the Germans 677,000.

TRENCH WARFARE

After the Battle of the Marne, Moltke was replaced by General von Falkenhayn as Chief of the German General Staff. The Germans had overrun almost all Belgium and about one tenth of France, including many of her most valuable mines and industrial areas. Falkenhayn was determined not to yield any of this territory, while at the same time he resolved to make the fighting as costly as possible to the Allies, from the point of view of manpower losses.

He realized that a well-constructed line of trenches would enable his armies to defend the conquered territory with the least demand upon manpower, and the least risk of heavy casualties. The Germans therefore began to dig themselves in. They constructed lines of deep trenches so that the soldiers were below surface level, safe from Allied machine gunners and riflemen. Deeper and larger dug-outs were made, securely roofed over, where the officers had their headquarters.

Long, twisting, communication trenches led far to the rear, and along these the supplies were brought up. In front of the trenches a maze of barbed wire entanglements was erected, so that no enemy could approach without first cutting a way through or flattening it out. Anyone attempting to do this would be subjected to murderous machine gun fire.

As the Germans withdrew, they were able to choose the most suitable ground for their line of trenches. They were almost always on higher ground, so that the Allies were forced to dig theirs in lower situations which were more liable to become water-logged. This was part of the reason why the German trenches were generally superior to those of the French and British. The Germans were also very thorough: their dug-outs were sometimes forty or fifty feet deep, shored up with three-inch planking, and well furnished. Behind the trenches they constructed a great network of light railways to bring up ammunition and supplies.

During the first winter, conditions in the Allied trenches were very bad. Captain P. A. Thompson describes them: '. . . our men lived in ditches half filled with mud and water. At first no attempt was made to revet (strengthen) the sides, and as time went on these sides kept slipping down and widening the trench, leaving more mud at the bottom. There they lived in bitter, biting cold, soaked to the skin; with mud in their nails, their hair, their eyes—mud

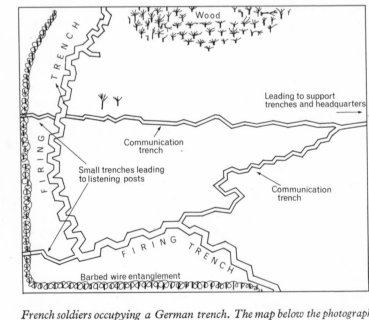

French soldiers occupying a German trench. The map below the photograph shows this sector of the trench system

British Tommies getting down to earth

everywhere. There each man made his dug-out, narrow as a grave, just big enough for him to crawl into, the earth walls sweating, a floor board to sleep on, with his overcoat as his only covering. Perhaps he was lucky enough to have a mess room eight feet square, roofed with corrugated iron which gave no real protection. But those who had never been buried beneath the debris of an explosion felt happy if they were under any sort of cover, even a piece of canvas. Those who had been buried once hated to be under anything.

Those dug-outs were the only homes they knew, and after standing up to their knees in slush all day in the firing trench, it was a tragedy to come back only to find that some shell had caused their dug-out to collapse.

Five yards or so to the rear of the support trench would be found the officers' mess—a dug-out some four or five yards square and five feet high, roofed with beams supporting wire netting covered with sand-bags. Those sand-bags were best filled with bricks or stones to detonate a 'whizz-bang' on contact, rather than let it penetrate and explode inside. If anything heavier than a 'whizz-bang' hit the roof, that dug-out was 'done in'.

As summer came on the trenches dried up, but they became fearfully infested with lice and rats. And they were stinking! Many dead bodies lay for months in No-man's land. Sometimes as they dug some new communication trench they would cut into a body, long dead. So they added to the awful stench the all-pervading odour of chloride of lime. . . .

And there they stayed, filled with the grimmest determination, yet longing past all expression that the war might soon be over; feeling no personal animosity for the fellows in the trench on the other side, fifty yards away; and seeing little glory in being horribly mangled by bomb or shell. . . .

Yet their sense of humour never departed, and as you made your way through "Plug Street Wood" you would be directed from Hyde Park Corner down Regent Street, and you would pass by dug-outs that were labelled as the Ritz or the Carlton.'*

By late autumn the two series of front line trenches stretched for hundreds of miles from the Swiss border to the sea. Between them lay No-man's land, a desolate area of mud and shell holes. It proved to be almost impossible to break completely through these lines of trenches, although millions of men were sacrificed in vain attempts to do so. For nearly four years this state of deadlock continued, and spades, barbed wire and machine guns became the chief weapons of war on the Western Front.

THE WAR AT SEA

The British had expected a great naval battle, in which they hoped to destroy the German High Seas Fleet and then to establish a close blockade of the German coast; but the ships of the German fleet remained in their ports.

On the open sea the Allies soon gained complete control. German merchant ships vanished from the high seas, being either captured or driven into neutral harbours, and the Allies were able to blockade the Central Powers, cutting off all trade by sea except in the enclosed Baltic, which was sealed off by minefields and the German submarines. Gradually, it was hoped, Germany would grow short of food and supplies essential for the war, and would be forced to give in. To prevent Germany from obtaining supplies through neutral countries, the Allies intercepted and searched neutral shipping, and

* From *Lions Led by Donkeys* by P. A. Thompson (Werner Laurie).

confiscated all goods that might be of any use for the war effort. There was great indignation in America, Holland, Denmark and other countries at this interference with their right to trade and to use the 'freedom of the seas'.

The Germans, too, tried to blockade Britain by mines and submarines. Since Britain depended so largely on imports of food and raw materials, Germany hoped to starve her into defeat. Mines were sown in Britain's shipping routes and left loose to drift in the North Sea.

On 28th August a few British destroyers were sent through the protective minefields into the Heligoland Bight, where they engaged the German patrols of cruisers and destroyers. The Germans gave

Admiral Beatty on the quarter deck of HMS Queen Elizabeth

chase, and the destroyers retreated, closely followed by the Germans, who sailed straight into the trap which Vice-Admiral Beatty had laid for them. He was waiting with his battle cruisers, and sank three German cruisers.

After this the German ships stayed more closely within their own waters until December, when their battle cruisers slipped out under cover of darkness and bombarded Scarborough and other English coastal towns.

Meanwhile a world-wide hunt was being conducted by the Allied navies. There were several powerful modern German warships in various parts of the world, and these did much damage to Allied shipping before the Allied navies were able to locate and settle with them. Thousands of troops were travelling to the European war zone from Canada, Australia, New Zealand, South Africa and India. All these needed protection from German submarines and raiding warships on many thousands of miles of sea routes; the Allied navies had an anxious time. Most of the biggest ships of the British Navy remained in home waters, in case the German Grand Fleet attacked across the North Sea.

Admiral von Spee, the German commander in the Pacific had two powerful cruisers and several smaller ships. Early in November he encountered a small British squadron off the coast of Chile. He sank the British cruisers *Good Hope* and *Monmouth*, with every man on board. Not a single German was killed. Von Spee put into Valparaiso for a few days; a group of Germans greeted him enthusiastically and presented him with flowers. Knowing that the British Fleet would be out for revenge, he accepted the flowers with the words: 'They will do for my funeral.'

A month later he met a much stronger British force at the Falkland Islands. Von Spee's ship sank with all hands; his companion ship continued to fight against hopeless odds, and then, completely helpless, opened the sea cocks and went down with her flag still flying.

Two German warships escaped into the Turkish waters of the Sea of Marmora. There they were able to bring pressure to bear upon Turkey, who agreed to enter the war on the side of Germany.

The entry of Turkey into the war was a serious blow to the Allies, as it closed the main route to Russia. By the end of the year Russia had almost run out of munitions, and was in urgent need of supplies from her Western allies.

The King exhorts volunteers to join the British army

One of the many posters showing young men what was expected of them

THE GROWING ARMY

The year was drawing to a close. In Britain the reality of the war was being brought home to the people. In many families the young men had joined up, while other families opened their doors to strangers, as troops in training were billeted in private houses throughout the country. The soldiers would march into the town and line up in the street. Then in twos and threes they would be assigned to the various houses. The boys and girls watched excitedly, their mothers anxiously, to see which of the khaki-clad men would be coming to them. Soon Highlanders and Northumberlanders, Welshmen and men from Lancashire were enlivening the quiet little towns of the south. The country roads rang with whistling and singing, as the men tramped along on their endless route marches. The drums and pipes stirred the hearts of boys too young to enlist.

The soldiers sang songs—not war songs or patriotic ones, but 'It's a long way to Tipperary' and 'Pack up your troubles in your old kit bag and smile, smile, smile.' They knew that they might be killed, and would probably be wounded—they had volunteered knowing this, but the songs they sang did not suggest any such things. They preferred:

> Send for the boys of the old brigade
> To set old England free,
> Send for my father, my sister, my brother,
> But for God's sake don't send me.

Soon the wounded began to appear, and men in blue uniforms, some blinded, some maimed and crippled, hobbled about on crutches, were pushed about in wheelchairs or sat about on the public seats. The call for more and more men to join the army became increasingly urgent. Everywhere, from walls and hoardings and the backs of buses, the face of Lord Kitchener, Secretary for War, stared at every man, and his accusing finger pointed at every man over the caption: 'Your country needs YOU'. Other posters exploited family ties. Before the end of the year more than a million men had volunteered, most of them willingly, but some driven by the reproaches of others. Some young women were always ready to give a white feather to men who looked as though they ought to be in the army, meaning that they were despised as cowards for not volunteering.

*Men
of the
German and British
armies*

THE ENEMY ABOVE AND WITHIN

Sudden wild scares swept the country: there was going to be an attack from the air, and every day people would gaze anxiously at the sky. For the moment, however, the skies were peaceful; air raids were still a thing of the future. Then a spy fever struck Britain. There were hundreds of German waiters, barbers and small shop-keepers in Britain, many of whom had lived in the country for twenty or thirty years. Suddenly they had all become, in the popular imagination, dangerous spies and enemy agents. In Brixton, Deptford and other places, crowds attacked their shops and houses, smashing windows and destroying property, dragging out the terrified victims who were lucky if they were handed over to the police without being beaten up.

Thousands of Germans and Austrians of military age were taken to detention camps in various parts of the country, most of them in the Isle of Man.

THE BROTHERHOOD OF MAN

Christmas came, but there were no signs of a speedy end to the war—unless the ordinary soldiers took matters into their own hands.

Before the war, members of the trade unions and other working men's organizations in many countries had called a congress to discuss whether it would be possible for them to prevent their governments from going to war. The ordinary people of Britain, Germany, France, Austria and Russia had no quarrel with one another, they wanted peace, better wages, better food and clothing, better homes. These could not be obtained by war, by harming the very customers who bought their goods and so enabled them to earn a decent wage. They had talked of strikes which would make it impossible for their governments to go to war. But war had come before anything had been decided. They had planned their next congress for August 1914, the very month in which the war had spread. It was to have met in Vienna, the capital of the first country to declare war. The congress never met. But some of the men in the trenches had not forgotten.

On Christmas Eve, in many places along the front line trenches, the British and French soldiers saw rows of little lights, and across the frozen mud of No-man's land came the sound of singing. Down in their trenches the Germans were singing carols. Then the Germans themselves appeared. They climbed out one by one, singing and waving lanterns, and moved towards the Allied trenches. Throwing down their rifles, the British and French soldiers climbed out, and went to meet their enemies, shaking hands and exchanging gifts and sharing cigarettes. For a few hours Christian peace reigned. But to the army leaders such behaviour was dangerous; it never occurred again.

German troops celebrating Christmas Day on the Eastern Front

Documentary Five

Trenches in Belgium

'*You must dig in*', General Foch insisted, '*It's the only way of staying out of sight and of avoiding losses.*' *His listeners were in agreement on the principle, but after a rather long silence General Wielmans objected that while this theory was sound in normal terrain, it could hardly be applied in Belgium where water is on a level with the ground and is found even in the smallest diggings. . . . Foch admitted that the problem was by no means easy to solve, but he went on to state that wartime circumstances sometimes call for the most drastic decisions, such as having soldiers standing in water in order to avoid an enemy barrage. The Belgian officers listened respectfully but could not help feeling that the French commander of the northern army group was not sufficiently acquainted with the very special conditions under which the Belgian troops had fought and suffered so far. . . .*

. . . General Foch concluded : 'To survive, nations must be ready to fight. It would be inconceivable for us to try to reconquer Belgium without having the Belgian Army at our side. As a soldier of the Republic I can assure Your Majesty that ours is a sacred cause, and that Providence will grant us victory.'

The King remained silent, but he clasped the general's hand very warmly. . . .

In the evening, after General Foch's departure, he ordered that 'Units holding outposts, edges or trenches, shall under no circumstance abandon their position. Neither the losses sustained, nor the threat of encirclement, nor the number of opposing enemy forces can authorize or justify any withdrawal.'

From SOUVENIRS DE 1914: *en Belgique aupres du roi des Belges* by General Brecard (Calman–Lévy)

Effects of the war on the people of Britain

There is something infinitely greater and more enduring which is emerging already out of this great conflict—a new patriotism, richer, nobler, and more exalted than the old. I see amongst all classes, high and low, shedding themselves of selfishness, a new recognition that the honour of the country does not depend merely on the maintenance of its glory in the stricken field, but also in protecting its homes from distress. It is bringing a new outlook to all classes. The great flood of luxury and sloth which had submerged the land is receding, and a new Britain is appearing. We can see for the first time the fundamental things that matter in life, and that have been obscured from our vision by the tropical growth of prosperity.

From a speech by Lloyd George at Queen's Hall on 19th September 1914

There is not a single person of German or Austrian birth, whether naturalized or not, employed in our establishments.

From an announcement published by the Ritz Hote

REFUSE TO BE SERVED BY AN AUSTRIAN
OR GERMAN WAITER
IF YOUR WAITER SAYS HE IS SWISS
ASK TO SEE HIS PASSPORT

Prominently boxed item in THE DAILY MAIL

This is no ordinary war, but a struggle between nations for life and death. It raises passions between nations of the most terrible kind. It effaces the old landmarks and frontiers of our civilization.

Winston Churchill in THE TIMES, 1st November 1914

A German view of Britain and the need for a submarine blockade

The Germans have always been at a disadvantage with regard to England, as they could never overcome their sentimental feeling of justice and delicacy, even when other feelings would be more suitable. We waste too much time on humane things, while our enemies regularly do us harm whenever and wherever they can. Now England is waging a 'business war' against us, hoping to crush us economically. We must therefore begin a systematic war of retaliation against British commerce. For this we possess the most effective tool—our submarines. Naturally this weapon must be employed not merely against hostile warships, but against all shipping under the enemy flag approaching British coasts. Towards an enemy like England—which knows no leniency where questions of reaching her aim are concerned, who with the greatest want of principle disowns the white race and fights shoulder to shoulder with coloured people—to such an enemy we need show no leniency. In the submarine Germany has an advantage which must be used with all determination.

From an official article in the BERLINER LOKAL-ANZEIGER
by Rear-Admiral Paul Schlieper

Christmas 1914

On Christmas day groups of men from both sides went out and met in No-man's land, and even visited each other's trenches. It was rather a shock to our men, who were dirty and had beards of several days' growth, but nevertheless expected to find their enemies half famished, to see instead that 'Jerry' was spic and span, well shaven, and possessing an abundance of cigars, and champagne. That day each side pressed cigars, drinks and souvenirs upon their enemies, and on that evening one of our colonels had great difficulty in inducing some of the enemy to return to their own trenches.

This spirit prevailed for some days afterwards, and various stories became current. How one of our Royal Engineers putting up barbed wire, borrowed a mallet from a neighbouring 'Jerry' who was similarly employed. In another place where parties from each side were putting up wire in front of their trenches, they agreed to put up one lot of wire midway between the opposing trenches to serve for both.

From LIONS LED BY DONKEYS by Capt. P. A. Thompson (Werner Laurie)

THE WAR OF ATTRITION

1914 ended in deadlock: on the Western Front neither side could be outflanked, and the most violent frontal attacks met with no real success. There was not even room for surprise—no attack could be made across the barbed wire entanglements without prolonged bombardment first, to flatten them out. In the east too, winter had slowed down activity, and the front seemed to be settling down to

Turkish troops going over the top

trench warfare. The Germans were short of manpower, the Russians lacked machine guns, rifles and ammunition. In fact, most armies at this time found themselves short of some types of ammunition. Since the army leaders in all the belligerent countries had expected the war to be a short one, none had prepared the huge capacity for munitions production which was needed for the continuous fighting on such a vast scale. Shells were sometimes in such short supply that the guns were rationed to a few rounds per day.

Now the army leaders could see little hope of quick victory, no way of breaking the deadlock.

The leaders of the navy pinned their hopes upon the blockade: slowly but surely, they thought, the shortage of food and essential goods would become acute in the Central Powers, as almost all

trade was cut off. But the blockade was a slow weapon—it would be years before the shortages would be so great that the enemy would be forced to surrender.

Trench warfare, with murderous frontal attacks, blockade and the slow starvation of the entire enemy nations—these seemed to many of the Allied leaders the only strategy for 1915—and 1916—and 1917 —and who knew for how much longer?

It was argued that as the Allies had a larger population than the Central Powers, if the combatants continued to kill one another off at roughly the same rate, when enough millions had been wiped out, the Allies would be left with overwhelming superiority, and so should win the war in the end. This was known as 'the war of attrition'.

This seemed to be the principle on which the High Command based their conduct of the war, and they could therefore contemplate the loss of a hundred thousand men in a few days fighting as the regrettable but necessary price of ultimate victory. Unfortunately, as Churchill said, the Allied losses were nearly double those of the Germans.

FIGHTING IN THE TRENCHES

When an attack was to be made, an artillery *barrage* was put over, and salvoes of shells were directed at the enemy front line, to destroy the barbed wire defences, to open up the trenches into a series of craters, and to smother the occupants of the dug-outs. Shrapnel shells followed, to wipe out the men whose defences had just been destroyed.

Immediately the guns ceased, the men went 'over the top' and charged across No-man's land, hoping that the wire would be properly flattened, and that there would be few of the enemy left alive in the trench. If this was not the case, they would be subjected to a withering machine-gun fire.

When an attack was expected, the front line trenches would be only thinly held, and as soon as they were captured, they would be heavily shelled in retaliation. A little way beyond would be other trenches, strongly held, and the same process would have to be repeated.

The theory behind this type of attack was that if only one kept it up long enough, the enemy's line would be completely pierced, and the cavalry would then advance through the gap created, fan out, cut the enemy's communications, and 'roll up' the whole front.

In practice, the attack almost certainly lost its momentum before a real breakthrough was achieved, and all that could be done was to re-dig the captured enemy trenches and consolidate the position. This would probably be a bulge into enemy territory, and so subjected to fire from the flanks as well as the front, and so more difficult to hold. As Churchill said of the German offensive in 1918: 'Every offensive lost its force as it proceeded. It was like throwing a bucket of water over the floor. It first rushed forward, then soaked forward, and finally stopped altogether, until another bucket could be brought.'*

A further development of trench warfare was mining. Teams of miners were formed, and they dug tunnels from the front line to a point below important objectives in the enemy line, and then blew them up. Mining and counter-mining became one of the most important features of trench warfare. After the Germans had introduced the use of poison gas, both sides fired gas shells before an attack.

Large scale attacks were made by the Allies in the spring of 1915: by the French in Champagne from January to March, by the British east of Rheims in March, by the French at Vimy in May–June and by the British at Aubers in May. The Germans made an attack at Ypres in April. In no case was a breakthrough achieved.

LLOYD GEORGE AND THE MINISTRY OF MUNITIONS

In May it was reported in England that shortage of high explosive shells had prevented the British from pressing home their advantage in an attack near Lille. There was anxiety and bitter criticism at home, and as a result a Ministry of Munitions was set up, and Lloyd George was appointed Minister. He was in office for a year, and during that time he transformed the British economy. He began with a requisitioned hotel, with no tables and no staff. By the end of the war the Ministry employed a staff of 65,000 and had over three million workers under its direction.

* From *The Great War* by W. S. Churchill (Newnes), p. 1133.

The Cabinet set up a committee to control the new Ministry. It met once only. Then Lloyd George took complete charge. He produced far more shells than the War Office asked for, but not enough for the army requirements. This did not happen until 1918.

Meanwhile the Ministry was turning out vast numbers of machine guns—the 1,330 with which the army started the war was increased by the manufacture of 240,506 more.

It was Lloyd George's Ministry of Munitions which produced the valuable Stokes light mortar which the War Office turned down. It was his Ministry which developed the tank, after Kitchener had dismissed it as 'a pretty mechanical toy'. The Ministry set up 218 national munitions factories and worked with 20,000 smaller ones which had hurriedly been adapted or built to meet the sudden

After a gas attack

demand. The Ministry took power to requisition all the supplies of
steel it needed. Male munition workers were paid high wages and
were exempt from call-up for the army.

NEW APPROACHES

Although the military leaders seemed content to batter away at the
enemy on the Western Front, and were now prepared to let the war
drag on until the enemy were exhausted, some leading men in the
Allied governments, particularly Winston Churchill, thought
differently. Could a weakness be found in the whole enemy position,
and a completely new plan be worked out? Could Germany be
attacked from the north or Austria from the south? Could Turkey be

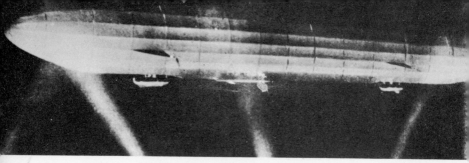

A zeppelin caught in the arc lights over London

forced to surrender by an assault on the Straits and Constantinople? This would open up communications again with the south of Russia. One of these plans, successfully carried through, might end the war in 1915.

The Germans, too, hoped to break the deadlock by some new stroke. Their best plan seemed to be to create a rift in the *Triple Entente* by persuading Russia to make a separate peace. To obtain this, the Germans offered Constantinople to Russia, although it was the capital city of their own ally, Turkey. But by secret treaty Britain and France had already agreed that Russia should have Constantinople—they were ready to give to Russia the very thing which they had been trying to prevent for a hundred years. The German attempt to split the Allies was unsuccessful.

The Germans also introduced a new weapon into the fighting on the Western Front—poison gas:

> *Gas! Gas! Quick, boys!—an ecstasy of fumbling,*
> *Fitting the clumsy helmets just in time,*
> *But someone still was yelling out and stumbling*
> *And flound'ring like a man in fire or lime.*
> *Dim through the misty panes and thick green light,*
> *As under a green sea, I saw him drowning.*
>
> *In all my dreams before my helpless sight*
> *He plunges at me, guttering, choking, drowning.**

This was written by Wilfred Owen, a poet who fought and was killed on the Western Front.

Soon the Allied soldiers were supplied with gas masks and no great victory was gained through the use of gas. The Germans made the mistake of trying it out on a small scale and so lost the advantage of a grand surprise attack.

* From *Dulce et Decorum Est*, in *Collected Poems* (Chatto & Windus).

German air raids on Britain were developed in 1915. The first raid by a single plane had been at the end of 1914. Now the night skies were bright with sweeping searchlight beams, seeking out German zeppelins and aeroplanes. Police paraded with placards saying POLICE NOTICE TAKE COVER. Windows were blacked out at night, and the policemen went round to see that no chinks of light would show the raiders where the towns were.

The results of the bombing were very slight. Did the Germans hope to cause panic? Did they think that fear of raids might make the people beg for peace? The only result was a greater determination than ever to beat the enemy.

THE DARDANELLES EXPEDITION

The Allies decided to make an attack on Turkey in the spring of 1915 in the Dardanelles. A successful assault on Turkey might have encouraged Greece, Bulgaria and Rumania to join the Allies. They were all enemies of Turkey, and stood to gain by her defeat. Italy would also be anxious to get a share of the Turkish Empire, and would have joined the Allies (see map on p. 67).

There were long delays, and the Turks under German leadership were able to build up strong defences. Landings were made at a very heavy cost in lives, and an Allied army clung to the barren tip of the peninsula of Gallipoli. Fierce attacks failed to gain much ground, and each side dug in. Trench warfare put an end to further advances.

THE SEARCH FOR NEW ALLIES

Meanwhile Germany was trying to persuade Bulgaria, Rumania, Italy and Greece to join in the war on her side. Bulgaria was particularly important, as the route from Germany and Austria to Turkey passed through her territory. Bulgaria, however, waited to see how the war in Gallipoli would turn out.

Rumania hoped to gain large areas from Austria–Hungary in Transylvania, which was largely inhabited by Rumanians, but she feared attack by Germany, and she too waited.

Greece was divided: King Constantine's sympathies were with Germany, but Venizelos, the outstanding Greek politician, wanted to join the Allies. Italy hoped to gain from Austria territory which was

German gunners, in gas masks, with a heavy Howitzer

largely inhabited by Italians, and she also wanted to gain control of the Adriatic Sea and much of its eastern shores. By the secret Treaty of London, in April 1915, the Allies promised Italy practically everything she wanted. Early in May she declared war on Austria-Hungary.

THE INVASION OF SERBIA

A big Allied attack in Gallipoli in August ended in complete failure. This decided Bulgaria that the Allies were going to lose the war, and she joined the Central Powers. Germany, Austria and Bulgaria then combined in an overwhelming attack on Serbia. In spite of bitter resistance, the whole country was overrun and thousands of defenceless people perished as the Bulgarians ravaged their country. In spite of the opposition of the King of Greece, the Allies decided to build up an army at Salonika; but it was too late to save Serbia.

THE CAPTURE OF WARSAW

There was no continuous and well-constructed trench line on the Eastern Front. At the end of February the Russians made a great advance, and in March they captured the huge fortress of Przemysl. After their failure to break through at Ypres in April, the Germans switched their offensive to the east with massed artillery. In June

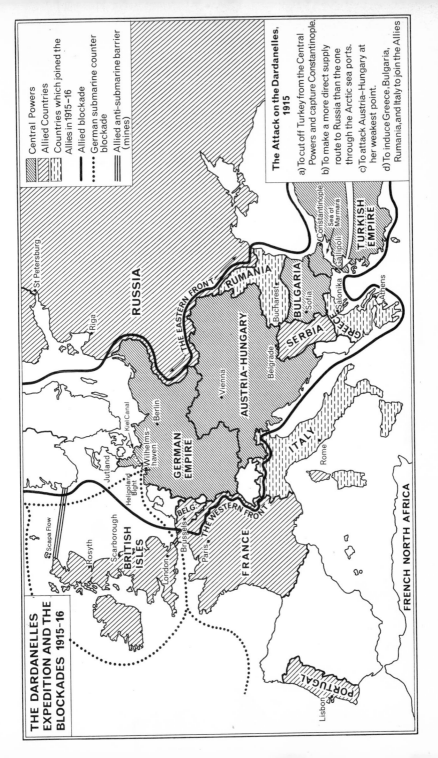

THE DARDANELLES EXPEDITION AND THE BLOCKADES 1915-16

Central Powers

Allied Countries

Countries which joined the Allies in 1915-16

Allied blockade

German submarine counter blockade

Allied anti-submarine barrier (mines)

The Attack on the Dardanelles, 1915

a) To cut off Turkey from the Central Powers and capture Constantinople.

b) To make a more direct supply route to Russia than the one through the Arctic sea ports.

c) To attack Austria-Hungary at her weakest point.

d) To induce Greece, Bulgaria, Rumania, and Italy to join the Allies

St Petersburg

RUSSIA

Riga

THE EASTERN FRONT

RUMANIA

Bucharest

BULGARIA

Sofia

SERBIA

Belgrade

GREECE

Salonika

Athens

Constantinople

Sea of Marmara

Gallipoli

TURKISH EMPIRE

Vienna

AUSTRIA-HUNGARY

Kiel Canal

Berlin

Wilhelms-haven

GERMAN EMPIRE

ITALY

Rome

Jutland

Heligoland Bight

BELG.

Brussels

THE WESTERN FRONT

Paris

FRANCE

Scarborough

BRITISH ISLES

London

Rosyth

Scapa Flow

FRENCH NORTH AFRICA

PORTUGAL

Lisbon

they re-took Przemysl and by August they had captured Warsaw, the capital of Russian Poland.

The Russians were very poorly equipped, many of the men being without rifles, and those who had them were often unable to use them through lack of ammunition. They were therefore forced to retreat continuously, but managed to extricate their main armies. At the end of September, Vilna fell to the Germans but, as they advanced, their lines of communication lengthened until it became so difficult to keep up the vast supplies needed that the advance ceased. The Germans, however, had made such rapid progress that they felt the complete defeat of Russia could not be far away.

In September 1915, leaders on the Western Front decided on a great offensive. Attacks were made by the French in Champagne and Vimy, and by the British at Loos. After huge losses the attacks petered out.

GALLIPOLI

In Gallipoli the situation appeared so hopeless that in December it was decided to withdraw all troops. This was done at night in complete silence, and in the morning the Turks found the trenches in front of them deserted.

The failure in Gallipoli ended the hope of a quick finish to the war. Russia remained almost cut off from her allies, doomed to fight without proper weapons and munitions, until she was faced with complete collapse. As Sir Winston Churchill said: 'The end of the Dardanelles campaign closed the second great period of the struggle. There was nothing left on land now but the war of exhaustion, not only of armies but of nations . . . only frontal attacks by valiant flesh and blood against wire and machine guns, 'killing Germans' while Germans killed Allies twice as often; calling out the men of forty, of fifty, and even fifty-five, and the youths of eighteen, sending the wounded soldiers back three or four times over into the shambles.'*

---

* From *The Great War* by W. S. Churchill (Newnes), p. 782.

Documentary Six

Trench warfare at close quarters

The C.O. told us that we were ordered to consolidate the new position at Hooge. He said we would have to dig in and wire all night, and that we must be prepared for a counter-attack.

The place reeked with the smell of decomposed bodies. They lay about in hundreds, on top of the parapets, in our trenches, in No-man's land, and behind the parados. The British dead mostly belonged to the 2nd York and Lancs, and the 2nd D.L.I. The dug-outs were full of dead Germans. . . .

Dawn broke at 4 a.m. . . . One could now make out the country all round perfectly, and what an appalling sight it was. Everywhere lay the dead. The ridge in our rear was covered with dead men who had been wiped out in the final assault of the German position : their faces were blackened and swollen from the three days' exposure to the August sun, and quite unrecognizable. Some of the bodies were badly dismembered : here and there a huddled heap of khaki on the brink of a shell-crater told of a direct hit. Haversacks, tangled heaps of webbed equipment, splintered rifles, and broken stretchers lay scattered about. The ground was pitted with shell-holes of all sizes. A few solitary stakes and strands of barbed-wire was all that was left of the dense mass of German entanglements by our artillery. Several khaki figures were hanging on these few strands in hideous attitudes. In front of us, in No-man's land, lay a line of our dead. . . . There was not a blade of grass to be seen in No-man's land or on the ridge, the ground had been completely churned up by the shells, and any of the few patches of grass which had escaped had been burnt up by the liquid fire.

. . . our trench was full of German dead. . . . They lay in the dug-outs, where they had gone to seek refuge from our guns, in fours and in fives. Some had been killed by concussion, others had had their dug-outs blown in on top of them and had suffocated. Our gunners had done their work admirably.

At 5 a.m. some shells fell all along our line. Then all was silent and we realised the meaning of those dozen shells which traversed our line from left to right, ranging shells for a pukka bombardment. Within fifteen minutes of the burst of the last shot, a steady bombardment started all along our line.

The enemy gunners carried out their work in a most systematic manner. They fired by a grouping system of five shells to a limited area, under 12 yards. Then they burst shrapnel over this area. This plan for shelling our position was undoubtedly successful, as three out of five shells hit our trench, obliterating it, blowing in the parapet on top of the occupants, or exposing them to a deadly hail from shrapnel shells. Our casualties were beginning to mount up.

From the diary of Captain F. Hitchcock, of the Leinster Regiment, relating to conditions in the Ypres salient on 11th and 12th August 1915 quoted in THE DONKEYS by Alan Clarke (Hutchinson)

The first use of gas

Soon those observers who were on points of vantage saw two greenish-yellow clouds creeping out across No-man's land in the French sector. These clouds spread laterally, joined up and, moving before a light wind, became 'a bluish-white mist, such as is seen over water-meadows on a frosty night' . . . people in the rear areas became aware of a peculiar smell and smarting of the eyes.

Then as the enemy artillery fire lifted, dense masses of fugitives came stumbling down the roads from the direction of Langemarck and Pilckem. Few of them could speak, none intelligibly, many were blue in the face, others collapsed choking by the side of the road. . . . At this time the mob was composed about equally of Tirailleurs, civilians and French-African troops, but it soon became thicker and more disordered as the first of the French artillery teams and wagons attempted to drive their way through those on foot.

The air was heavy with fear, with the stark panic of the unknown. . . . It was obvious that something very serious had happened, although for about an hour the 'seventy-fives' of French divisional artillery could still be heard. Then, at about 7 p.m., these too suddenly and ominously ceased fire.

From THE DONKEYS by Alan Clarke (Hutchinson)

A trench song

If you want to find your sweetheart,
* I know where he is,*
I know where he is, I know where he is,
If you want to find your sweetheart,
* I know where he is,*
Hanging on the front line wire.

Headquarters staff

. . . the Headquarters staff 'never witnessed, not even through a telescope, the attacks it ordained, except on carefully prepared charts where the advancing battalions were represented by the pencil which marched with ease across swamps and marked lines of triumphant progress without the loss of a single point. As for the mud, it never incommoded the movements of this irresistible pencil.'

Lloyd George, quoted in THE EUROPEAN POWERS 1900–45
by Martin Gilbert (Weidenfeld & Nicolson)

Shortage of shells

. . . the want of an unlimited supply of high explosive shells had been a fatal bar to the success of the British attempt to storm the heights commanding Lille, which, if taken by the Allies, would render the German salient at La Bassée untenable.

From the report of the Military Correspondent of THE TIMES,
14th May 1915

VERDUN

1916 was the year in which opportunity lay most strongly with the Germans. They ended 1915 in a most favourable position: Allied attacks on the Western Front had failed, and the Germans had suffered far fewer losses than the Allies. In the east, great German victories had forced the Russians back until all Poland and Galicia were cleared of Russian troops. Serbia had been completely overrun, and the Allies had been forced to give up their attack on the Dardanelles.

General von Falkenhayn, German Commander-in-Chief, had a very difficult choice to make: should he carry out a sort of Schlieffen Plan in reverse, just hold the Western Front, and press home the victorious advance in the east; drive Russia to complete defeat and withdrawal from the war, so gaining the rich food-producing lands of the Ukraine; then surround Rumania and force her to enter the war and so gain control of her great supplies of corn and oil; then drive right through western Asia, break the blockade and go on to threaten the British Empire in India? Or should he revert to the ideas of 1914 and try to knock out France by destroying her armies in an all-out attack?

He decided to attack in the west, and he massed the German troops for a great assault on the famous fortress of Verdun. 'The French will bleed themselves white,' he said, 'to prevent the fall of such a fortress.' He was right. 'They shall not pass!' became the watchword of the French defenders, and in the fighting which extended from February, through March, April, May and June, nearly half a million Frenchmen were killed, wounded or captured. The German losses were not much more than half that number.

But if Falkenhayn was right in this, he had nevertheless made the wrong choice. The Allies still had sufficient resources to launch a tremendous attack upon the German lines on the river Somme during July, while in the east far worse had befallen the German cause.

New recruits for the French army

RUSSIA'S RECOVERY

During the winter a wonderful recovery had been made by the Russians. Much of the Trans-Siberian railway had been double-tracked, and a new railway brought to Murmansk. Munitions poured in from Japan, Britain, France and the U.S.A., while Russia's own factories were multiplying their production. A tremendous assault was planned on the southern part of the Eastern Front, and on 4th June the attack began. In a week 100,000 prisoners were taken, and by the end of the month nearly three-quarters of a million Austrians had been killed, wounded or captured. In the northern part of the Front the Germans were forced to retire to keep in line with the defeated Austrians. Encouraged by these victories, Rumania decided to declare war on Austria–Hungary, and prepared to invade Transylvania.

There was great satisfaction among the Allies: Germany would be denied the great quantities of Rumanian corn and oil, while another half a million men would be put into the field against her.

THE BATTLE OF JUTLAND

Morale in Germany was sagging badly, and the Kaiser's naval advisers thought a victory at sea would do much to restore confidence. Admiral Scheer knew that in a battle between the British Grand Fleet and the German High Seas Fleet, Britain's much greater strength offered him little hope of survival, certainly none of victory. He therefore hoped to entice a part of the British navy into battle with his whole forces. If he could inflict heavy losses on the British in two or three such actions, he could then risk a final battle on more or less equal terms.

At the end of May a number of U-boats were sighted in the North Sea, but they did not appear to be attacking merchant ships. The Admiralty were suspicious. On 30th May they picked up wireless messages which could not be deciphered, but which suggested that orders had been given to the German navy for a major operation. Instructions were sent to Admiral Sir John Jellicoe to leave Scapa Flow with his great force of battleships, and to Vice-Admiral Sir David Beatty to leave Rosyth with the battle cruisers and to concentrate their forces in the North Sea (see map on p. 67).

Meanwhile the German Admiral Hipper had been ordered to sail with his battle cruiser fleet out of Wilhelmshaven. The plan was to engage the British fleet which was expected to come out to meet him, and to draw it into the minefields and within reach of Scheer's High Seas Fleet which followed Hipper out to sea. German submarines would be operating off Scapa Flow and Rosyth, to attack the British ships as they came out.

Things went as Scheer expected, and the Battle of Jutland began with a running fight between Hipper's and Beatty's battle cruisers with their accompanying light cruisers and destroyers. Neither side knew that the enemy's main fleet was near. Scheer's reconnaissance zeppelins failed to sight the British fleets before they were recalled, as the weather was too bad, while the British Admiralty had misinterpreted messages by which they should have known that Scheer's main fleet was at sea. Only one British reconnaissance seaplane went up, and that was forced down and its message failed to reach the Admiral. It was considered too rough to risk launching any other seaplanes. Communications between the British ships and the Admiral were very unsatisfactory. Methods were inefficient, and commanders of several ships failed to send reports.

Beatty, however, succeeded in signalling to Jellicoe that the battle was in progress, and Jellicoe steamed south at full speed.

As soon as he contacted Beatty's fleet, Hipper moved southwards at high speed, to lead Beatty into the German High Seas Fleet. The German gunnery proved to be much better than that of the British battle cruisers, and the German ships had thicker armour, and better safety devices to prevent the spread of fire. Two British battle cruisers were sunk, and Beatty sent his destroyers in to attack. Then he became aware of the approach of the German High Seas Fleet, and he turned northwards to lure Scheer towards Jellicoe's great force.

ADMIRAL JELLICOE'S DILEMMA

When Scheer realized that he was faced by Britain's entire battleship strength, he turned away to avoid envelopment, while Jellicoe was deploying his fleet for an attack. Meanwhile there was a sharp action between the advance forces of the two main fleets, and a duel between Rear-Admiral Hood's 3rd Battle Cruiser Squadron and the German battle cruisers. Another British battle cruiser was sunk. Hidden by the mist and smoke, the German High Seas Fleet disappeared, but in an attempt to slip past the British, it came into contact with Jellicoe's force again, and a furious cannonade took place. Fearing total defeat, Scheer ordered his battle cruisers and destroyers to go in to the attack, to screen his withdrawal with the main fleet.

Jellicoe was faced with a very serious decision. If he pressed on he would run grave risks of heavy losses through torpedo attacks from the German destroyers. He dared not run this risk. The destruction of the British main fleet would have been absolutely disastrous. The vast quantities of food, raw materials and munitions which Britain obtained from abroad, and which were essential for the war effort, would be cut off. Supplies to the British armies in France and elsewhere would be ended. All help from the U.S.A. would stop, and the possibility that America would join the Allies would end. Starvation and ruin would have followed, and Britain herself would have been open to invasion.

The destruction of the German High Seas Fleet, on the other hand, would not have been so serious for Germany. It had played

HMS Lion, Beatty's Flagship, on fire after a hit on one of her gun turrets

only a minor part in the war, and had been quite unable to prevent the Allied blockade. It had, however, ensured the safety of the bases from which the German submarines operated in their attacks on Allied shipping. It also protected north-western Germany from a possible Allied attack. Neither Jellicoe nor Scheer would have been justified in risking the destruction of his country's main fleet.

There was therefore tremendous responsibility upon Jellicoe. He must not allow himself to be drawn into a full-scale battle unless he was almost certain of victory. As Winston Churchill said: 'Jellicoe was the only man on either side who could lose the war in an afternoon.'*

Jellicoe therefore took evasive action to avoid the destroyer torpedo attack, and was then unable to make contact with the High Seas Fleet, which had again disappeared in the mist and smoke. He decided not to risk a night action, and by morning the whole German fleet had slipped away to its home ports. The full-scale battle between the two navies had not taken place, much to the regret of the British at home.

A GERMAN VICTORY?

The Germans claimed a great victory. Ninety-nine German ships had sunk nearly 112,000 tons of British shipping, while 151 British ships had sunk 62,000 tons of German. Of 60,000 British officers and men 6,097 were killed; the 36,000 Germans lost only 2,551.

* From *The Great War* by W. S. Churchill (Newnes), p. 837.

The President of Rumania signs the peace treaty in a tense atmosphere

There was great rejoicing in Germany, and disappointment in Russia where it was realized that there was little hope of an Allied breakthrough to the Baltic, which would have opened up a way for the much needed supplies.

In spite of her heavier losses, however, the British navy was still nearly twice as strong as the German, and it still retained command of the sea. For the rest of the war the Germans did not risk another great sea battle, and the German naval authorities realized that the only way to break the British blockade was by intensive submarine warfare.

German morale continued to improve. The great Russian advance had been stopped, and as soon as the Rumanians invaded Transylvania, Bulgarian, Austrian, Turkish and German forces invaded Rumania from south and west. By the end of the year all the Rumanian armies were beaten, and Rumania withdrew from the fighting. All her supplies of corn and oil fell into German hands after all.

CONSCRIPTION IN BRITAIN

The prospect of further massive attacks on the Western Front during 1916 led to a change of policy in the raising of troops in Britain. Hitherto Britain had relied upon volunteers, and many British people felt that she had no need for the continental system of conscript armies. So many British soldiers had already been killed and seriously wounded, however, that early in 1916 the Government decided to bring in conscription. This meant that all unmarried men of the right age could be made to join the army—the time of the volunteers was over. Later, married men were also conscripted.

There was some opposition to conscription, mainly on religious grounds. Some Christians, including most of the Quakers or Friends, thought it wrong to kill at any time, and they refused to join the army. Others, mainly socialists, believed that the state had no right to force men to fight for a cause they did not believe in. These men were called conscientious objectors, and were brought before local tribunals. If they were considered to be genuine, they were offered work of national importance instead of service in the army. Some joined first aid units and went to the Front, where they ran the same risks as the soldiers, but took no part in the fighting. Others worked on the land, producing the food which was vitally necessary.

Some C.O.s, as they were called, refused to do anything which would help the war effort, and they were sent to prison, and often very harshly treated.

IRELAND

Other opposition to England's part in the war came from a number of people in Ireland. Before the war there had been much bitterness in Ireland, when the British parliament was preparing to give Ireland Home Rule, with a parliament of its own. Most of the Irish were Roman Catholics, and the people of Ulster, who were Protestants, were ready to rebel. They would fight to prevent the Home Rule Bill from putting them, as they thought, at the mercy of the Catholic majority.

On the outbreak of the war, the Home Rule Bill was dropped, and most of the Irish people, both Protestant and Catholic, supported the war, and many of them joined the British army. Some of the southern Irish, however, thought that England's difficulty was Ireland's opportunity, and they began to plan a rebellion. Sir Roger Casement went to Germany to try to persuade the Germans to land arms and men in Ireland.

A rising was planned for Easter 1916. The Germans did not think there was much chance of success, and a German submarine landed Casement in Ireland with the object of calling off the rebellion, but before he could contact his companions he was captured.

Most of the Irish plotters also were doubtful and went home, but about 2,000 of them captured the Post Office and other buildings in Dublin, and proclaimed the Irish Republic. After five days of fighting they were forced to surrender. The leaders were shot; Sir Roger Casement was taken to London, found guilty of treason and hanged. Thousands of Irishmen were sent without trial to concentration camps in England. There was much bitterness in Ireland at this treatment. England claimed that she was fighting the war for the freedom of small nations such as Belgium, so why not freedom for Ireland? The Irish rebels claimed that they *had* been fighting for the freedom of the Irish nation. Britain, however, was fighting desperately to stave off possible defeat, and hoped for ultimate victory. If freedom for the Irish endangered that victory, then freedom must wait, and all resources must be devoted to the war effort.

WOMEN DURING THE WAR

As more and more men were taken for the army, many of their jobs had to be carried out by women, jobs which before the war nobody would have thought of asking women to do; jobs which women would never have thought of doing, though sometimes they were jobs which some women would have been only too pleased to do—if the men had let them. Soon there were women car drivers, tram and bus conductors, sweeps, bakers, railway workers, munition workers and factory workers of all kinds. Although not actually allowed to become soldiers and fight in the trenches, many women got as near to it as possible, by joining women's Army, Navy and Air Force Auxiliaries, and doing much of the administrative work of the forces, which released the men for the fighting line.

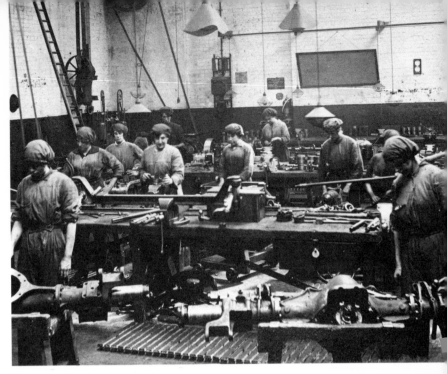

Women working for the war effort

THE SOMME

The Allies began their great offensive on the Somme on the Western Front in July. After their huge losses in the defence of Verdun, the French could not take a large part, and the main share of the fighting and dying was this time borne by the British.

There was no new plan, merely the hope of piercing the German lines by wave after wave of frontal attacks, and then wheeling round to north and south behind the German lines, so forcing a general retreat. There was no attempt at surprise—the need for a preliminary intense bombardment made this impossible. When the men went 'over the top' and stormed what was left of the enemy trenches, there were still large numbers of Germans armed with rifles and machine guns in the partially wrecked trenches, and in other defensive positions. The attacking waves wilted and withered away. Fresh waves of attackers followed, until large enough numbers reached the German positions to force their defenders back.

Day after day and week after week the slaughter and struggle went on. With the autumn came the rain, and the whole area became a sea of mud. In Winston Churchill's words: 'A vast sea of ensanguined mud, churned by thousands of vehicles, by hundreds of thousands of men and millions of shells, replaced the blasted dust. Still the struggle continued. Still the remorseless wheels revolved. Still the auditorium of artillery roared. At last the legs of men could no longer move; they wallowed and floundered helplessly in the slime. Their food, their ammunition lagged behind them along the smashed and choked roadways.'*

At the end of months of heroic struggle, the Germans had given up a few miles of useless territory; but there were always more defences beyond, and the Allies never got far enough through to turn the German flank. The German losses were something over 500,000, but those of the British and French reached the appalling total of 800,000.

By this time the maps at home, with the little flags, were nearly all forgotten—the flags had stayed so long in the same positions that interest was lost. All the gains of a battle like the Somme were so small that no change was needed in the positions of the flags.

Marching up to the front through a passage in the barbed wire

* From *The Great War* by W. S. Churchill (Newnes), p. 908.

THE FIRST LANDSHIPS

At this battle of the Somme a new weapon was used, and a wonderful chance missed. Ever since the autumn of 1914 experiments had been going on in an attempt to get a machine or vehicle which could crush barbed wire entanglements and cross lines of trenches. Several ideas had been tried out: one had huge wheels forty feet in diameter, others had caterpillar traction. The War Office was not at all impressed either with the need for such an invention, or with the suggested models. Strangely enough it was the Admiralty, not the Army, which first pressed on with this attempt to solve the problem of victory on land. It was Winston Churchill, First Lord of the Admiralty, who ordered the first of these 'landships'. And so the first tank was made.

At last Army Headquarters expressed a mild interest. Lloyd George, Minister of Munitions, was keen and fifty were ordered. Had they been made in thousands, there might have been a real breakthrough. It would have been better not to have used them until the following year, when the value of surprise and large numbers would probably have been overwhelming. Instead, a few were used towards the end of the battle. Then 'One single tank on

British tanks, captured and re-named, being put through their paces

this first occasion, finding the attacking infantry held up in front of Flers by wire and machine guns, climbed over the German trench, and travelling along behind it, immediately and without loss forced its occupants, 300 strong, to surrender.'*

In the British parliament there was great dissatisfaction with the war situation, and towards the end of 1916 Lloyd George became Prime Minister instead of Asquith. He was a man of tremendous energy, enthusiasm and optimism. There was no disaster which he did not meet cheerfully, and from which he did not hammer out some constructive and successful action.

1916 ended, a year of lost opportunities on both sides, but with German control extended over a much larger area. In spite of this, the Allied blockade was slowly strangling the Central Powers; but there was still no overwhelming victory in sight for either side.

A motor bus converted into a mobile pigeon loft for service on the Western Front. Pigeons were used extensively for getting messages from the Front to H.Q. Dogs were also used.

* From *Lions Led by Donkeys* by P. A. Thompson (Werner Laurie), p. 230.

Documentary Seven

Verdun

'Verdun!' The name was continually on our lips in the East from the beginning of February in this year....

I must admit that the attack on Verdun was also a bitter disappointment for us, for the enterprise meant that the idea of a decision here in the East had been finally abandoned. . . . Doubts gradually began to prevail: Why should we persevere with an offensive which exacted such frightful sacrifices and, as was already obvious, had no prospect of success?

From OUT OF MY LIFE by Marshal von Hindenburg (Cassell)
Supreme Commander on the Russian Front

At dawn on December 15th our artillery positions . . . were heavily bombarded with gas shells. The French infantry advanced shortly before 11 a.m. . . . Fighting went on till late in the evening, but all our struggles were in vain. . . . This second defeat before Verdun was marked by a disproportionately high total of prisoners lost. . . . The enemy's communiqué claimed 11,000 prisoners, mostly unwounded, from all five of our divisions....

The spirit of our troops had declined to a marked degree . . . to a considerable extent their morale and power of resistance was unequal to the demands placed upon them by their onerous task....

The mighty drive of the battles for Verdun in 1916 was at an end! . . . Small wonder if this ill-starred end to our efforts wrung the hearts of the responsible commanders.

From MY WAR EXPERIENCES by Crown Prince William of Germany
(Hurst & Blackett)

Jutland

By 1600 hours we were at close grips with the enemy. His fire was phenomenally accurate . . . a bloodstained Sergeant of Marines appeared on the bridge. He was hatless, his clothes were burnt and he seemed to be somewhat dazed. I asked him what was the matter; in a tired voice he replied: ' "Q" turret has gone, sir. All the crew are killed, and we have flooded the magazine.' I looked over the bridge. The armoured roof of 'Q' turret had been folded back like an open sardine tin, thick yellow smoke was rolling up in clouds from the gaping hole and the guns were cocked up awkwardly in the air.

From an account by Lieutenant W. S. Chalmers,
who was on the *Lion's* bridge,
in THE BATTLE OF JUTLAND by G. Bennett (Batsford)

The Indefatigable *was hit by two shells . . . both appeared to explode on impact. Then there was an interval of about thirty seconds; at the end the ship blew up, commencing from forward. The explosion started with sheets of flame followed by a dense, dark smoke cloud which obscured the ship from view. All sorts of stuff was blown into the air, a 50-ft steamboat being blown up about 200 ft, apparently intact though upside down.*

From an account by an officer on board the *New Zealand*,
in THE BATTLE OF JUTLAND by G. Bennett (Batsford)

They hurled themselves recklessly against the enemy line. A dense hail of fire swept them all the way. Hit after hit struck our ship. A 15-inch shell pierced the armour of 'Caesar' turret and exploded inside. Lieutenant-Commander von Boltenstern had both legs torn off and nearly the whole gunhouse crew was killed. The shell set fire to two cordite charges; the flames spread to the transfer chamber where they set fire to four more . . . the burning cases emitted great tongues of flame which shot up as high as a house; but they only blazed, they did not explode as had been the case with the enemy. This saved the ship, but killed all but five of the seventy men inside the turret . . .

From an account by Von Hase
on board the *Derfflinger*, one of the German battle cruisers,
in THE BATTLE OF JUTLAND by G. Bennett (Batsford)

Jellicoe on the taking of risks

It is absolutely necessary to look at the war as a whole, and to avoid being parochial, keeping our eyes on the German fleet only. What we have to do is to starve and cripple Germany, to destroy Germany. The destruction of the German Fleet is a means to an end and not an end in itself. If in endeavouring to destroy the German Fleet we run risks which may prejudice our success in the greater object of destruction of Germany, those risks are too great.

From THE BATTLE OF JUTLAND by G. Bennett (Batsford)

A neutral view of Jutland

The German Fleet has assaulted its jailor, but is still in jail.

From a New York newspaper

The Somme

At 7.30 a.m. the hurricane of shells ceased as suddenly as it had begun . . . a series of extended lines of British infantry were seen moving forward from the British trenches. The first line appeared to continue without end to right and left. It was quickly followed by a second line, then a third and fourth. They came on at a steady pace as if expecting to find nothing alive in our front trenches . . . when the leading British line was within 100 yards, the rattle of machine-guns and rifle fire broke out from along the whole line of craters. Some fired kneeling so as to get a better target over the broken ground, while others in the excitement of the moment, stood up regardless of their own safety to fire into the crowd of men in front of them.

Red rockets sped up into the blue sky as a signal to the artillery, and immediately afterwards a mass of shells from the German batteries behind tore through the air and burst among the advancing lines. Whole sections seemed to fall, and the rear formations, moving in close order, quickly scattered. The advance rapidly crumbled under this hail of shells and bullets. . . .

The British soldier, however, has no lack of courage, and once his hand is set to the plough he is not easily turned from his purpose. The extended lines, though badly shaken and with many gaps, now came on all the faster. . . . Again and again the extended lines of British infantry broke against the German defences like waves against a cliff, only to be beaten back. It was an amazing spectacle of unexampled gallantry, courage and bulldog determination on both sides.

From DIE SCHWABEN AN DER ANCRE by Matthaus Gerster,
quoted in THE GREAT WAR by Winston Churchill (Newnes)

The experimental use of tanks

I was so shocked at the proposal to expose this tremendous secret to the enemy upon such a petty scale, and as a mere make-weight to what I was sure could only be an indecisive operation, that I sought an interview with Mr. Asquith.

From THE GREAT WAR by Winson Churchill (Newnes)

The effects of the blockade

Excepting the very wealthy and those who have stored quantities of food for the 'siege', every German is undernourished. A great many people are starving. The head physician of the Kaiserin Augusta Victoria Hospital in Berlin stated that 80,000 children died in Berlin in 1916 from lack of food. . . .

But starvation under the blockade is a slow process, and it has not yet reached the Army. When I was on the Somme battlefields last November . . . the soldiers were not only well fed, but they had luxuries which their families at home did not have. Two years ago there was so much food at home the women sent food boxes to the front. Today the soldiers not only send but carry quantities of food from the front to their homes.

From GERMANY, THE NEXT REPUBLIC?
by Carl W. Ackerman (Hodder & Stoughton), an American journalist
who was in Germany at the end of 1916

GERMAN ADVANCES

In 1917 changes in the war situation took place on a vast scale. In January, Germany announced unrestricted submarine warfare against Britain: any ship approaching Britain was liable to be sunk without warning. It would often be impossible to rescue survivors. Protests from neutral countries were ignored; Britain must be reduced to submission at all costs.

In February nearly half a million tons of shipping were sunk, in March over half a million, in April 849,000 tons. Losses at this rate would reduce Britain to starvation and helplessness in a few months.

France and Britain also began 1917 with a desperate effort. They planned a great attempt to smash a way through the German lines in the west. After an advance of a mile or two the attack was halted; over 100,000 men had been lost. There was bitter disappointment. The French armies had fought bravely for nearly three years and suffered appalling casualties. Now they were near to breaking point: their patience and their hopes of victory were exhausted. There were widespread mutinies: thousands of soldiers left their positions and set out for Paris, to demand that peace should be made, and the slaughter stopped.

Meanwhile the British made violent attacks in Flanders, to try to capture Ostend and Zeebrugge from which some of the German submarines operated, but without success.

ALLIES LOST AND GAINED

In March another heavy blow struck the Allied cause. Revolution broke out in Russia. The Tsar abdicated, and a government was set up under Kerensky, a moderate socialist. He tried to continue the war against Germany, and launched an offensive, but, as Lenin the Russian Communist revolutionary said, the soldiers voted for peace with their feet. In thousands they deserted and made their way home, to make sure that they obtained their share of the land which was being taken from the nobles by the peasants and shared out.

Lenin, who was in exile in Switzerland, believed that if he could gain control of the revolutionary government in Russia, he would be able to withdraw Russia from the war. Then he thought the people of Germany, Austria, France and Britain would all follow

British soldiers on Passchendaele ridge during the battle of Flanders

the Russian example: there would be revolution everywhere, the war would end, and there would be universal peace.

The German leaders saw their opportunity: if Lenin gained control in Russia, the war in the east could be ended, and they could bring all their forces against the Western Allies. They were confident that they could prevent revolution spreading to Germany. They therefore gave Lenin secret passage from Switzerland across Germany to Russia, so that he could lead the revolution there. He arrived in April 1917 and immediately began to plan for a Bolshevik take-over.

If Britain and France were losing one ally, they soon gained another. In starting their unrestricted U-boat campaign, the Germans made their second fatal mistake. The first had been the invasion of Belgium, which had brought Britain into the war. This second colossal blunder gained her another enemy—the United States of America.

The Germans realized that the sinking of neutral ships might bring the U.S.A. into the war against them, but they expected to bring Britain to her knees before any large-scale help could arrive from America. In any case they hoped to sink most of the ships

A Russian soldier trying to stop his comrades deserting

carrying troops and supplies which America might send. They were engaged in a desperate race against time.

The United States did not hope to gain territory or wealth from Germany. For a long time her President, Woodrow Wilson, had done his best to keep America out of the war, but gradually feeling against Germany had grown, particularly over the sinking of neutral ships. Also, the Americans had lent vast sums to the Allies. They did not want to see them lost in an Allied defeat.

In his message to the American Congress, calling upon it to declare war on Germany, President Wilson said: 'The peace of the world is involved, and the freedom of its peoples . . . the world must be made safe for Democracy, for the rights and liberties of small nations.'

Many months had to pass, however, before the men could be trained, and the strength of America placed on the scales opposite the Central Powers.

SOCIALIST ATTEMPTS AT PEACE

Meanwhile, Kerensky's attempt to launch an offensive on the Eastern Front failed completely and he asked the Allies for permission to make a separate peace with Germany. The Allies refused. Some Russian socialists then proposed an international conference of socialists from Germany, Austria, Russia, France and Britain at Stockholm to discuss ways of arriving at a negotiated peace.

The Germans agreed to attend. The French government refused to grant passports, and English seamen refused to take the British delegates; so the conference came to nothing. To the Russians it appeared that the wishes of ordinary people counted for nothing— the leading people in each country wanted the war to go on—they wanted not peace, but complete victory, and the complete destruction of their opponents. Increasing numbers of people in Britain and France were coming to think the same—it was a 'bosses' war, where ordinary people were being sacrificed for profits; but there was no mass movement, no attempt at revolution outside Russia.

In Russia, Kerensky arrested many Bolshevik leaders, and Lenin went into hiding in Finland. Then Kornilov, the Russian Commander-in-Chief tried to crush the revolution altogether, including Kerensky himself. Kerensky released the Bolsheviks and armed the factory workers. Many of Kornilov's men deserted or went over to the Bolsheviks, who were then able to take over the city of Petrograd almost without opposition. The members of Kerensky's government were arrested, and Kerensky himself fled.

Lenin, as head of the Bolshevik government, called for an end to the war on all fronts. He invited all the governments to give up any land they had conquered during the war, and also all their colonies. The new peace was to be a fair one for all nations and peoples. The secret treaties by which the Great Powers had agreed to share out among themselves the lands of weaker peoples were published, much to the embarrassment of the British, French, Italian and German governments. The Bolsheviks hoped that the people of all countries would see that they were being exploited by their rulers, and rise in revolution everywhere.

These Bolshevik invitations were refused absolutely by all the governments. In France, socialists who wanted peace negotiations were accused of treachery and arrested. The war went on; but the Bolsheviks began negotiations with Germany for peace in the east, and the Germans began transferring men and guns to the Western Front. Peace was eventually made at Brest-Litovsk on 3rd March 1918, and Western Russia and the Ukraine passed into German control.

A giant U-boat in the North Sea

CONVOYS

Meanwhile Britain was desperately fighting the U-boat menace. Mines, nets, decoy ships and other devices were used, but sinkings continued at a fearful rate. Sir Maurice Hankey and a number of younger naval officers suggested to Lloyd George, the Prime Minister, that by sailing British ships in convoy the losses could be reduced. This would mean that all merchant vessels would sail in groups, protected by naval escorts. Admiral Sir John Jellicoe and the senior naval officers said it would be out of the question. It was argued that a convoy was a much bigger and easier target for the U-boats and that the whole convoy would be forced to sail at the speed of the slowest ship.

In early autumn, however, in spite of the strongest opposition, Lloyd George insisted that the convoy system should be tried. The loss of shipping dropped from 600,000 to 200,000 tons per month.

RATIONING

The shortage of food was very serious, and to eke out supplies a system of rationing was started, so that all people would get a share of the most important foods. People spent many hours a day queuing at food shops. There was scarcely any butter, and margarine was used instead. Beans and other things were ground up and mixed with wheat flour to make 'war bread', which was dark in colour. Potatoes were so short that many people went daily to every shop within reach which might possibly have any, queuing at each in the hope that at one of them they might get a pound or two. Seed potatoes were cut into little pieces for planting, and sometimes even potato peelings were planted.

Parks were dug up and food crops planted. Hundreds of thousands of people who had never gardened before took allotments and grew their own food.

The appearance of the countryside changed: woods and forests were cut down, as shipping space could not be spared to import timber. Canadian lumberjacks came to Britain to organize the tree felling.

ALLIED SETBACKS

Still another disaster befell the Allies in 1917. In October the Italians were routed at Caporetto, losing 800,000 men. British and French troops which could ill be spared were hurried to Italy to help her to recover.

In only two minor places on the fighting fronts was there anything but gloom or defeat for the Allies at the end of 1917. In Palestine, General Allenby had taken Jerusalem from the Turks, and on the Western Front at Cambrai, tanks enabled the British to penetrate the German line to a depth of six miles. But these were very small gleams of hope with which to meet the expected onslaught in 1918, when the Germans would have all the troops and resources released by the ending of the war with Russia.

A CONTRAST INDEED! BRITISH AND ENEMY CIVILIAN FOOD-SUPPLIES.

DRAWN BY OUR SPECIAL ARTIST, W. B. ROBINSON.

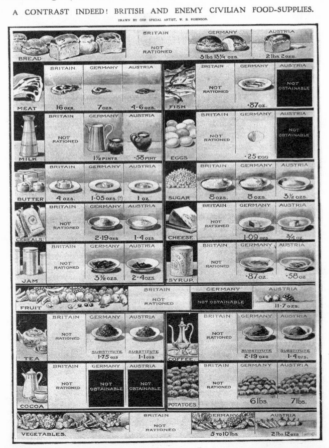

The effect of the blockades upon Britain and the Central Powers—a page from 'The Illustrated London News', March 1918

Documentary Eight

The Russian revolution

The 23rd of February was International Women's Day. . . . It had not occurred to anyone that it might become the first day of the revolution. However, in spite of all directives, the women textile workers went on strike. . . . Thus the fact is that the February Revolution was begun from below, the initiative being taken of their own accord by the most oppressed and downtrodden part of the proletariat—the women textile workers.

On the following day the movement doubled. The slogan 'Bread!' was crowded out or obscured by louder slogans 'Down with Autocracy'. . . .

The soldiers of the Volynsky regiment were the first to revolt. The training squad—that is the unit specially relied on to put down the insurrection—had refused to march out, its commander was killed. . . . They rushed into the neighbouring barracks, 'calling out' the soldiers, as strikers do. The Moscow regiment joined the uprising, not without inner struggle. The monarchist command impotently fell away from the solider mass, and either hid in the cracks or hastened to change its colours. The Czarist garrison of the capital, numbering 150,000 soldiers was dwindling, melting, disappearing. By night it no longer existed.

Can it be that that was the whole resistance put up by the redoubtable Russian Empire in the face of mortal danger! Yes, that was about all.

From HISTORY OF THE RUSSIAN REVOLUTION by Leon Trotsky (Gollancz)

Dear comrades, soldiers, sailors and workers. I am happy to greet in your persons the victorious Russian revolution, and greet you as the vanguard of the world-wide proletarian army . . . the piratical imperialist war is the beginning of civil war throughout Europe . . . world-wide socialism has already dawned . . . Germany is seething . . . any day now the whole of European capitalism may crash. The Russian revolution accomplished by you has prepared the way and opened a new epoch. Long live the world-wide socialist revolution.

From a speech by Lenin on his arrival at Petrograd in April 1917

The Provisional Government is deposed. . . . The causes for which the people were struggling—immediate democratic peace, abolition of the landlord's right to the land, labour control of industry, and a Soviet form of government—are now all guaranteed.

Long live the revolution of Workers, Soldiers and Peasants!

PROCLAMATION OF THE MILITARY REVOLUTIONARY COMMITTEE, 7th November 1917

The American entry into the war

We have no quarrel with the German people. We have no feeling toward them but one of sympathy and friendship. It was not upon their impulse that their Government acted in entering this war. It was not with their previous knowledge or approval. . . .

We have no selfish ends to serve. We desire no conquest, no domination. We seek no indemnities for ourselves, no material compensation for the sacrifices we shall freely make. We are but one of the champions of the rights of mankind . . . we shall fight . . . for democracy, for the right of those who submit to authority to have a voice in their own government, for the rights and liberties of small nations, for a universal domination of right by such a concert of free peoples as shall bring peace and safety to all nations and make the world itself at last free. . . .

From the speech by President Woodrow Wilson, 2nd April 1917

The first American troops in Paris

The rear was brought up by an enormous motor-bus load of the first American soldiers from the ranks to pass through the streets of Paris.

The crowds overflowed the sidewalks. They extended from the building walls out beyond the kerbs and into the streets, leaving but a narrow lane through which the motors pressed their way slowly. . . . From the crowded balconies and windows overlooking the route, women and children tossed down showers of flowers and bits of coloured paper. . . .

Old grey-haired fathers of French fighting men bared their heads and with tears streaming down their cheeks shouted greetings to the tall, thin, grey-moustached American commander who was leading new armies to the support of their sons.

From AND THEY THOUGHT WE WOULDN'T FIGHT
by Floyd Gibbons (Doubleday)

Food shortages in Britain

At Wrexham a big farm-wagon laden with potatoes already weighed into shillingsworths was brought into the square by agriculturalists who at once proceeded to sell them to all comers. The wagon was surrounded by hundreds of clamouring people, chiefly women, who scrambled on to the vehicle in the eagerness to buy. Several women fainted in the struggle, and the police were sent for to restore order.

From THE OBSERVER, 8th April 1917

THE TIMES *of 10th December 1917 listed the following as in short supply in London : sugar, tea, butter, margarine, lard, dripping, milk, bacon, pork, condensed milk, rice, currants, raisins, spirits, Australian wines.*

The food queues continue to grow. Outside the dairy shops of certain multiple firms in some parts of London women begin to line up for margarine as early as 5 o'clock on Saturday morning, some with infants in their arms, and others with children at their skirts. Over a thousand people waited for margarine at a shop in New Broad Street in the heart of the city, and in Walworth Road in the south-eastern side of London the queue was estimated to number about 3,000. Two hours later 1,000 of these were sent away unsupplied.

From THE TIMES, 17th December 1917

Convoy tactics

At 7 p.m. we sighted a cloud of smoke. I immediately steered towards it and soon discovered that we were near a southward-bound convoy, which comprised eight ships coming from the Shetlands, probably from Lerwick. The ships were sailing in a perfect straight line, which we always thought impossible for commercial vessels, the more so as they were of different sizes. Every ten minutes, the convoy changed course by about twenty degrees behind its leader. Four escort vessels, fanned out before the convoy, provided it with light, and two destroyers were zigzagging on both sides. The entire convoy gave the impression of a fleet of well-trained warships.

From SECHS JAHRE U-BOAT FAHRTEN by Johannes Spiess (Reimar Hobbing)
a German U-boat commander

The use of aircraft

All of our pilots and observers were doing splendid work. Everywhere we were covering the forward movement of the infantry, keeping the troops advised of enemy movements and enabling the British artillery to shell every area where it appeared concentrations were taking place. Scores of counter-attacks were broken up before the Germans had fairly launched them. . . . First of all our machines would fly low over the grey-clad troops, pouring machine-gun bullets into them or dropping high exposive bombs in their midst. Then the exact location of the mobilisation point would be signalled to the artillery, so that the moment the Germans moved our guns were on them.

From WINGED WARFARE by William A. Bishop (Hodder & Stoughton)

I have seen the grey-clad German troops throw themselves downward into open shell holes and dig feverishly with clawing fingers as we swooped in pairs upon them, our fire enfilading their position; gunners drop their occupation about the gun emplacements to scatter into shelter; horses turn and gallop off in terror dragging swaying waggons on the shell-holed roads until they turned them over in the wayside ditch; marching troops scatter in confusion to avoid our hail of lead.

From INTO THE BLUE by Captain Norman MacMillan (Jarrolds)

THE FOURTEEN POINTS

In 1918 the Germans made their supreme effort on the Western Front. At last the danger and frustration of war on two fronts was over, and all Germany's strength could be concentrated in the west.

The British armies, on the other hand, were weakened and greatly reduced in numbers by the continuous fighting of 1917, even when strengthened with every man that could be scraped together in Britain from the elderly, the youths, the wounded and the sick.

The Allies' main hope was that they would be able to hold on until massive American help arrived. In January President Wilson stated, in his Fourteen Points, the terms on which America was prepared to make peace. Belgium was to be freed, and Alsace and Lorraine were to be returned to France. The peoples of Austria–Hungary, the Balkans, the Turkish Empire and western Russia were to be freed to set up their own national governments. No other lands were to be taken from any country. There was to be a League of Nations, where all international problems could be settled peaceably, with no secret treaties.

The Allied governments accepted Wilson's Fourteen Points. Most of the war-weary people of Europe welcomed President Wilson's words with enthusiasm and relief. Here at last was the hope of real peace. But the German government was counting on decisive victory, and had no interest in peace on such terms. Preparations for the final assault proceeded.

THE FINAL GERMAN OFFENSIVE

It began on 21st March. The Germans attacked on the river Somme with overwhelming force. Their losses were heavy, but wave after wave of reserves continuously made them good. The British were outnumbered by three to one. It was impossible to hold the line and a retreat began.

Ludendorff, the German Commander-in-Chief hoped to over-whelm the British armies, crumple their line in a couple of days and drive them back upon the sea. His troops succeeded in breaking through, and they advanced about twenty-five miles, but then the task of repairing road and rail communications, and of bringing up supplies proved to be too difficult, and by 4th April they were halted. The first German offensive of the year had failed.

On 9th April the Germans struck again, this time against the British in Flanders. Again the British were flung back. After retreating for three days, Field Marshal Haig determined to yield no more ground, and he issued his famous order of the day: 'There is no other course open to us but to fight it out. Every position must be held to the last man. There must be no retirement. With our

Sir Douglas Haig being saluted and admired

backs to the wall and believing in the justice of our cause, each one of us must fight to the end. The safety of our Homes and the Freedom of mankind alike depend upon the conduct of each one of us at this critical moment.'

The British troops stood fast. More and more German reserves were thrown into the battle, and as British battalions were wiped out, fresh reinforcements closed the gaps. The line edged backwards but did not break. By the 18th the most violent stage of the battle was over, but the British had lost over 300,000 men, and the Germans 350,000.

THE ALLIED ADVANCE

Throughout May a great German attack on the French was expected, but the French did not know where. On 27th May it came, and on the first day the Germans broke through to a depth of twelve miles. In a few days they were once more on the Marne, and their long-range guns were firing shells into Paris. But now for the first time the Americans entered the battle in force. The retreating French soldiers were filled with new hope, and the Germans, who had not expected American intervention in such strength, were halted. Their contempt for the Americans rapidly diminished.

The Germans made two more assaults, and the battle hung in the balance, but everywhere the tide was turning and the German advance was stopped.

After their long and bitter withdrawal, the British now prepared to counter attack. On 8th August the tanks led Canadian, Australian and British troops in a shattering assault. Within two hours 16,000 prisoners and 200 guns were taken. Ludendorff wrote: 'August 8th was the black day of the German army.'

The Allied attack was extended. Soon the whole German line was moving back, fighting fiercely all the way. By 3rd September the retreat came to a halt, as the Germans reached the strongly fortified Hindenburg Line. Tremendous battles raged in the north, centre and south. The Hindenburg Line was pierced and broken. The whole Allied line again advanced.

News of the Allied victories on the Western Front spread quickly. The Allied armies at Salonika advanced against the Bulgarians. The heart had gone out of Bulgarian resistance, and at the end of

September they agreed to disband their army and to return all conquered territory.

At the same time the whole state of Austria–Hungary was breaking up. The subject peoples were setting up governments of their own in Allied countries, in preparation for a return to Austria to take over territory for their own independent nation states. The Turks withdrew from the war.

ARMISTICE

In October the Germans asked for an armistice, to stop the fighting while peace terms could be arranged. They announced that they were now willing to accept President Wilson's Fourteen Points.

First, Wilson demanded that they should withdraw from all invaded territory. This they agreed to do, and also ended their submarine campaign. He also said that he could not negotiate with the German emperor, and warned that the terms of the armistice would make it impossible for the Germans to renew the war. To Ludendorff this sounded little better than unconditional surrender, and he wished to fight on, but the German government had now decided to give in, and Ludendorff was dismissed.

The formidable organization of the German state was breaking up with startling suddenness: there was mutiny in the navy, revolution in Berlin and panic in the court. The Kaiser fled to Holland, and on 9th November Germany was proclaimed a republic.

The Allies were now willing to grant an armistice. On 11th November at 11 a.m. it came into force. For the first time for nearly four and a half years the guns were silent.

By the armistice terms the Germans surrendered thousands of guns and war planes, most of their army transport, all their submarines and almost all their navy. They were to withdraw from the left bank of the Rhine. Until the final peace terms were agreed, the Allied blockade was to go on, though a few food ships might be allowed through. This was a terrible decision, for not only were the people of central Europe suffering severely from lack of food, but hospital supplies and other necessaries were exhausted.

The final peace terms were to be settled at the Peace Conference at Versailles.

Documentary Nine

Ludendorff's offensives

The enemy's first position was quickly captured at all points. By evening the infantry of the divisions of the first wave, closely followed by their escort batteries, had penetrated to an average depth of six kilometres into the enemy's defensive system.

With ruthless energy the 18th Army's attack was continued during the night. . . . I shall never forget the scenes which I witnessed during these days. For the first time after more than two years of weary defence in the waste of trenches in the Western theatre of war the hour of liberation had struck and the command had gone forth to Germany's sons to strike for final victory in the open field. As if shaking off some horrible nightmare my infantry had risen from its trenches and crushing all resistance with unexampled vigour had broken through the enemy's defensive system. . . .

Among us marched long columns of captured Englishmen, worn out and with the mark of battle upon them, but also with the proud and self-reliant bearing peculiar to that nation . . .

From MY WAR EXPERIENCES by Crown Prince William of Germany
(Hurst & Blackett)

Low Allied morale

The German victory and especially the ease and rapidity with which it was achieved had a depressing effect on the Allied morale. It was the third great battle in which the Germans in a few days had broken through the Allied line to a depth which the French and British offensives had never reached after weeks and months of laborious and costly effort. The prisoners and guns captured by the enemy in each of these battles exceeded the highest record of the Allies in any of their great offensives . . .

. . . when the French were at the first assault swept out of Kemmel—a position which for years had been well behind the British front line—doubts began to creep into minds which hitherto had been confident of the undiminished proficiency of the French Army. The heavy defeat sustained by the French on the Chemin des Dames and the Aisne and the poor fight put up by their divisions, which enabled the enemy at one blow to advance within 40 miles of Paris, created for the time being a sense not only of despondency but of something tantamount to dismay.

From WAR MEMORIES by David Lloyd George (Odhams)

The effect of American troops

I have been seeing a good deal of Americans lately, and I must say, speaking from my own experience, our idea of what American men are like was quite wrong! Those we are working with are quiet, unassuming, practical fellows. Entirely unlike the fashionable Yankees we used to see in London following in the wake of some loud-voiced Yankee beauty!

Sir Douglas Haig in a letter to Lady Haig,
quoted in THE PRIVATE PAPERS OF DOUGLAS HAIG (Eyre & Spottiswoode)

The sudden appearance and dramatic entrance of the 2nd and 3rd Division into the shattered and broken fighting lines and their dash and courage in battle produced a favourable effect upon the French poilu. Although in battle for the first time, our men maintained their positions and by their timely arrival effectively stopped the German advance on Paris. It must have been with a decided feeling of relief that the worn and tired French soldiers retreating before vastly superior numbers, caught sight of Americans arriving in trucks at Meaux and marching thence on foot, hats off, eagerly hurring forward to battle. And the Germans, who had been filled with propaganda depreciating the American effort and the quality of our training, must have been surprised and disconcerted by meeting strong resistance by Americans on different points of this battle front.

From MY EXPERIENCES IN THE WORLD WAR by John J. Pershing
(Hodder & Stoughton)

Tanks in action, August 1918

Four hundred tanks in line of battle. Good going, firm ground, wheel to wheel, and blazing, brilliant weather. . . . Mark V Stars were to set off first, crash through the barbed wire aprons, bridge the trenches with their immense length, and amble leisurely along the trench system, dealing death and retribution by the way. The speedier Mark V's were to pass through to the second objective and mop up there; and finally, the nimble Whippers, to hound and pound the retreating enemy as he limbered up and beat it hot-foot. . . .

The front line now. A low parapet of earth looms ahead. . . . Now, a few wavering bayonets protrude. Swing her round. The epicycles behave beautifully. Round she slews, broadside on, to the enemy trench. The right six-pounder roars. A flash illuminates the dusky cabin as a canister of shrapnel is poured on the huddling field-greys. We trip merrily on, the six-pounder volleying shell after shell into the trench, and the two Hotchkiss machine gunners raking fore and aft as the Germans run for it.

From THE EIGHTH OF AUGUST by L. G. Morrison
(The Fighting Forces Magazine)

German morale crumbles

Early on August 8th, in dense fog, rendered still thicker by artificial means, the English, mainly with Australian and Canadian divisions, and the French attacked between Albert and Moreuil with strong squadrons of tanks . . . they penetrated deep into our positions. . . .

The report of the staff-officer I had sent to the battlefield . . . perturbed me deeply. . . . I was told of deeds of glorious valour, but also of behaviour which, I openly confess, I should not have thought possible in the German Army; whole bodies of our men had surrendered to single troopers or isolated squadrons. Retiring troops, meeting a fresh division going bravely into action had shouted out things like 'Black-leg' and 'You're prolonging the war', expressions that were to be heard again later. The officers in many places had lost their influence and allowed themselves to be swept along with the rest.

From LUDENDORFF'S OWN STORY by Erich von Ludendorff (Hutchinson)

The troops' reaction to news of the armistice

One can easily imagine the joy of our brave soldiers. . . . Yet they did not show their joy outwardly by shouts or songs, as one could have expected. . . . Every man among the victors retained his composure and self-control in these solemn moments, but the attitude of our vanquished enemies was quite different. At 11 o'clock sharp, they suddenly surged out of their trenches, shouting and flourishing a red flag, and carrying big signs with the word 'Republic' written on them. Many Germans wore a tricolour cockade on their caps. They were all eager to engage in conversation with our soldiers but, to their intense surprise, were disdainfully ignored by them. . . . Having been rebuffed by our men, the Boches began celebrating the armistice in their own trenches and in their own way. Throughout the entire sector, they threw grenades away, blew up the ammunition dumps. . . . They also began to sing merry songs and played instruments, apparently not realising that the armistice meant their country's complete collapse, the deepest humiliation ever sustained by Germany. True, they were badly misinformed by their leaders, so that they did not believe that their country was defeated militarily. They had been told that the armistice had been concluded mainly because revolution had broken out in Germany, and was spreading in the Allied countries too.

FROM MEMOIRES DE LA SOCIETÉ D'EMULATION DU DOUBS by G. Gazier

---

THE DIFFICULTIES OF PEACE

Three men dominated the Peace Conference at Versailles: President Wilson of the U.S.A., Prime Minister Georges Clemenceau of France and Lloyd George of Britain. No Russian representative was invited, nor were any of the defeated countries allowed to attend.

President Wilson wanted a just peace, so that no country would feel that it had been treated unfairly, and so want its revenge later. He wanted every nation to be free to have its own government. Above all he wanted a league of all nations, so that all could talk over their differences peaceably, and so avoid all war in the future.

Clemenceau wanted to keep Germany down, and make her so weak that she could never be a danger to France again. The cry of all the French people was 'Never again!'. Clemenceau had no room for Wilson's 'Fourteen Commandments' as he called them. 'God gave us His Ten Commandments and we broke them,' he said, 'Wilson has given us his Fourteen Points and we shall see.'

Lloyd George wanted to make Germany pay for the great damage caused by the war, but he also wanted to get back to normal trading as soon as possible. Britain was a country whose prosperity depended upon trade, and she therefore wanted the countries with which she traded to be prosperous. Among these were the defeated countries.

Clemenceau agreed to the League of Nations because he hoped it could be used to keep Germany weak. Wilson agreed to some things which he thought unjust because he hoped that they could be put right later through the League of Nations.

THE EFFECTS UPON GERMANY

After long arguments the peace terms were drawn up and presented to the Germans. All her colonies were to be taken from her and were declared to be Mandates, which were to be ruled by various Allies on behalf of the League of Nations. Germany was to have only a very small army and navy, and no submarines or military aircraft. She was to return Alsace and Lorraine to France, and to give up territory to the new country of Poland. She was to pay huge sums of reparations to compensate all the Allies for all damage done during the war. She was to admit that Germany alone had been guilty of causing the war.

The German delegates were bitterly disappointed and angered at the terms. 'This is not the just peace we were promised,' they protested. But they were disarmed and helpless; there was intense distress as a result of the Allied blockade which was still in force. They signed under protest.

Other treaties made Austria and Hungary into small separate countries, and created several new countries out of the old Austria-Hungary and out of western Russia. Turkey lost all her empire.

President Orlando of Italy, Lloyd George, Clemenceau and President Wilson during the conference at Versailles

THE AMERICAN REACTION

President Wilson then returned to America to get the agreement of the American government to the treaties, but he was met with a shattering blow. The American Senate refused to accept the treaty with Germany, and refused to join the League of Nations. Wilson had suffered many disappointments in Paris, but this was the bitterest of all. He began an intensive speaking tour of the country, trying to persuade his people to accept his beloved League of Nations. 'If the United States does not join the League,' he said, 'the war will have to be fought all over again.'

Depressed and worn out, President Wilson's health suddenly broke and the control of American policy passed to others. A separate treaty was made with Germany, and the U.S.A. withdrew from close contact with Europe. France became even more sceptical of the League, since the American withdrawal threatened the effectiveness of the Rhineland Demilitarized Zone which France had very reluctantly accepted instead of an armed frontier with Germany.

THE EFFECTS UPON BRITAIN

In Europe the treaties were put into effect. The war and the peace treaties had brought many changes, but no sign of lasting peace.

The only European Great Power who could feel fairly satisfied with the result was Britain, who had achieved the destruction of the German navy, and the control of some of the German colonies, some of which had also been obtained by British dominions—the Union of South Africa gained German South West Africa, and Australia part of New Guinea. Britain also received many German merchant ships, to replace those sunk by German submarines; but since this meant that she no longer needed to build ships herself, there was unemployment and distress among British shipbuilders.

It was no easy matter to find a satisfactory way of making Germany pay for the cost of the war, and the whole question of reparations was postponed, and dragged on for years, embittering the relations between the countries concerned. The war had brought something approaching chaos in economic affairs, and the stability of pre-1914 was never restored. Many thought that, as the Kaiser was responsible for starting the war, he should be brought to justice. Holland, however, allowed him to stay, and he died there in 1941.

THE NEW REPUBLICS

Another difficult problem was that of fixing the national frontiers of the new republican states, and of the old ones out of which they were carved. In many areas people of different nationalities were inextricably mixed, and it was inevitable that some minorities should be left under foreign rule.

The reconstituted Poland contained large areas which had been German, and which had many German-speaking inhabitants. The Germans in Bohemia were included in the new Czechoslovakia— they did not like being 'under' the Czechs, but at the same time they wanted to remain part of Bohemia, the Czech heartland.

Austria, reduced to its small German-speaking area, wished to join Germany, but the Allies would not allow this. These were matters that a future Germany would want to change—Germany was still a Great Power and, with the increase in the number of small states, she was likely to become more powerful than ever. No wonder France remained afraid of a resurgent Germany, and did her best to weaken her.

The new Poland also included much territory previously Russian, and many people of Russian and Ukrainian nationality.

In spite of these and other minorities, the settlements of the peace treaties left far fewer people in Europe under foreign governments than ever before in European history.

EAST AND WEST

The Bolshevik government of Russia was treated first as an enemy, and then as an outcast. Allied troops were sent to aid the counter-revolutionary leaders, and the revolution was turned into a bitter civil war. When the Bolsheviks finally drove out all their enemies, the Great Powers refused to recognize their government. Russia was thus pushed into isolation, and the foundations were laid for the division of the world into hostile East and West, communist and capitalist, which has caused so much of the world's trouble ever since. The fears that Bolshevism would soon spread to other parts of Europe were not immediately realized. Only in Hungary and Bavaria were there 'red' regimes, and then only for a very short time. Europe outside Russia remained capitalist. The empires were gone, and many of the monarchies; they were replaced by republics, but these were equally antagonistic to the Russian communists.

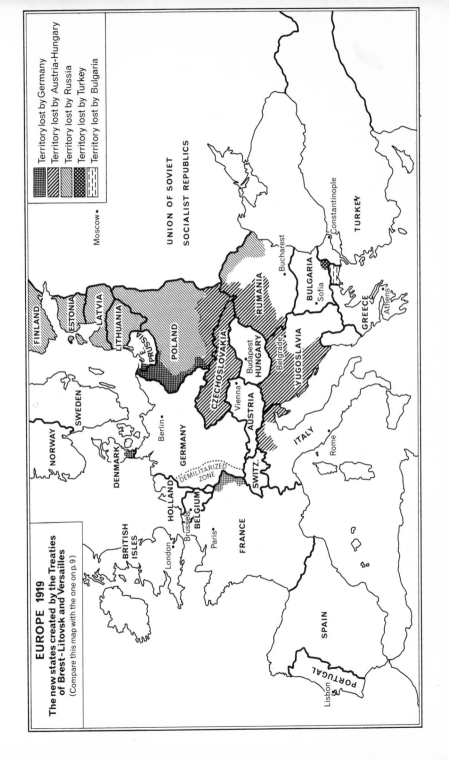

EUROPE 1919

The new states created by the Treaties
of Brest-Litovsk and Versailles
(Compare this map with the one on p.9)

Territory lost by Germany
Territory lost by Austria-Hungary
Territory lost by Russia
Territory lost by Turkey
Territory lost by Bulgaria

UNION OF SOVIET
SOCIALIST REPUBLICS

Moscow •

FINLAND

ESTONIA

LATVIA

LITHUANIA

E. PRUSSIA

POLAND

CZECHOSLOVAKIA

RUMANIA

Bucharest •

BULGARIA

Sofia •

Constantinople

TURKEY

GREECE

Athens •

YUGOSLAVIA

Belgrade •

HUNGARY

Budapest •

Vienna •

AUSTRIA

SWITZ.

ITALY

Rome •

DEMILITARIZED
ZONE

GERMANY

Berlin •

DENMARK

SWEDEN

NORWAY

HOLLAND

BELGIUM

Brussels •

London •

BRITISH
ISLES

FRANCE

Paris •

SPAIN

PORTUGAL

Lisbon •

A LEAGUE OF NATIONS?

The League of Nations came into existence without the U.S.A.,
Germany or Russia. Its main purpose was to keep the peace, but how
was that to be done? Should the Versailles settlement be open to
revision, or should it be firmly implemented? History has shown
that The League could keep the peace only as long as its chief
members wished to remain peaceful—and this was unlikely to be the
case for very long: there were many factors likely to lead to conflict.
The defeated nations were bitter and resentful. France was anxious
and frustrated. Italy was dissatisfied at being robbed of what she had
considered her rightful spoils of victory. President Wilson's fears
were indeed justified. Twenty years later the war had to be fought
all over again.

Peace in 1918, but for how long?

Documentary Ten

Clemenceau and the Peace Treaty

. . His principles for the Peace can be expressed simply. In the first place, he was a foremost believer in the view of German psychology that the German understands and can understand nothing but intimidation, that he is without generosity or remorse in negotiation, that there is no advantage he will not take of you, and no extent to which he will not demean himself for profit, that he is without honour, pride or mercy. Therefore you must never negotiate with a German or conciliate him : you must dictate to him. On no other terms will he respect you, or will you prevent him from cheating you. But it is doubtful how far he thought these characteristics peculiar to Germany, or whether his candid view of some other nations was fundamentally different. His Philosophy had, therefore, no place for 'sentimentality' in international relations. Nations are real things, of which you love one and feel for the rest indifference—or hatred. The glory of the nation you love is a desirable end—but generally to be obtained at your neighbour's expense. . . . Prudence required some measure of lip service to the 'ideals' of foolish Americans and hypocritical Englishmen ; but it would be stupid to believe that there was much room in the world, as it really is, for such affairs as the League of Nations. . . .

From ESSAYS IN BIOGRAPHY by J. M. Keynes (Hart–Davis)

The signing of the Peace of Versailles

. . . Wilson and Lloyd George are among the last. They take their seats at the central table. The table is at last full. Clemenceau glances to right and left. He makes a sign to the ushers. . . . There is then an absolute hush, followed by a sharp military order. The Gardes Républicains at the doorway flash their swords into their scabbards with a loud click. 'Faites entrer les Allemands,' says Clemenceau in the ensuing silence.

. . . And then, isolated and pitiable, come the two German delegates, Dr. Müller, Dr. Bell. The silence is terrifying. Their feet upon a strip of parquet between the savonnerie carpets echo hollow and duplicate. They keep their eyes away from those two thousand staring eyes, fixed upon the ceiling. They are deathly pale. They do not appear as representatives of a brutal militarism. . . . It is all most painful.

They are conducted to their chairs. Clemenceau at once breaks the silence. 'Messieurs,' he rasps 'la séance est ouverte.' He adds a few ill-chosen words. 'We are here to sign a Treaty of Peace.' The Germans leap up anxiously when he has finished, since they know that they are the first to sign. . . . There is general tension. They sign. There is general relaxation. Conversation hums again in an undertone. The delegates stand up one by one and pass onwards to the queue which waits by the signature table.

Suddenly from outside comes the crash of guns thundering a salute. It announces to Paris that the second Treaty of Versailles has been signed. Through the few open windows comes the sound of distant crowds cheering hoarsely.

. . . Only one delegate remained to sign. . . . There was a final hush. 'La séance est levée,' rasped Clemenceau. Not a word more or less.

We kept our seats while the Germans were conducted like prisoners from the dock, their eyes still fixed upon some distant point of the horizon.

From PEACEMAKING 1919 by Sir Harold Nicholson (Methuen)

Some provisions of the Versailles Treaty

Article 119. *Germany renounces in favour of the Principal Allied and Associated Powers all her rights and titles over the overseas possessions.*

Article 160. *By a date which must not be later than March 31, 1920, the German Army must not comprise more than seven divisions of infantry and three divisions of cavalry.*

Article 189. *All fortified works, fortresses and field works situated in German territory to the west of a line drawn fifty kilometres to the east of the Rhine shall be disarmed and dismantled.*

Article 198. *The armed forces of Germany must not include any military or naval air forces.*

Article 231. *The Allied and Associated Governments affirm and Germany accepts the responsibility of Germany and her allies for causing all the loss and damage to which the Allies and Associated Governments and their nationals have been subjected as a consequence of the war imposed upon them by the aggression of Germany and her Allies.*

From A HISTORY OF THE PEACE CONFERENCE OF PARIS
by H. W. V. Temperley (Oxford)

The Covenant of the League of Nations, 1919

The High Contracting Parties,

In order to promote international co-operation and to achieve international peace and security

by the acceptance of obligations not to resort to war,

by the prescription of open, just and honourable relations between nations,

by the maintenance of justice and a scrupulous respect for all treaty obligations in the dealings of organized peoples with one another,

Agree to this Covenant of the League of Nations. . . .

Article 8. *The Members of the League recognize that the maintenance of peace requires the reduction of national armaments to the lowest point consistent with national safety and the enforcement by common action of international obligations.*

Article 11. *Any war or threat of war, whether immediately affecting any of the Members of the League or not, is hereby declared a matter of concern to the whole League, and the League shall take any action that may be deemed wise and effectual to safeguard the peace of nations. In case any such emergency should arise, the Secretary-General shall on the request of any Member of the League forthwith summon a meeting of the Council.*

It is also declared to be the friendly right of each Member of the League to bring to the attention of the Assembly or of the Council any circumstance whatever affecting international relations which threatens to disturb international peace or the good understanding between nations upon which peace depends. . . .

Article 12. *The Members of the League agree that if there should arise between them any dispute likely to lead to a rupture, they will submit the matter either to arbitration or to inquiry by the Council, and they agree in no case to resort to war until three months after the award by the arbitrators or the report by the Council.*

Article 13. *The Members of the League agree that whenever any dispute shall rise between them which they recognize to be suitable for submission to arbitration and which cannot be satisfactorily settled by diplomacy, they will submit the whole subject-matter to arbitration. . . .*

Article 15. . . . *If a report by the Council is unanimously agreed to by the members thereof other than the Representatives of one or more of the parties to the dispute, the Members of the League agree that they will not go to war with any party to the dispute which complies with the recommendations of the report.*

If the Council fails to reach a report which is unanimously agreed to by the members thereof, other than the Representatives of one or more of the parties to the dispute, the Members of the League agree that they will not go to war with any party to the dispute which complies with the recommendations of the report.

Article 16. *Should any Member of the League resort to war in disregard of its covenants under Articles 12, 13, or 15, it shall* ipso facto *be deemed to have committed an act of war against all other Members of the League, which hereby undertake immediately to subject it to the severance of all trade or financial relations, the prohibition of all intercourse between their nationals and the nationals of the covenant-breaking State, and the prevention of all financial, commercial or personal intercourse between the nationals of the covenant-breaking State and the nationals of any other State, whether a Member of the League or not.*

It shall be the duty of the Council in such case to recommend to the several Governments concerned what effective military, naval or air force the Members of the League shall severally contribute to the armed forces to be used to protect the covenants of the League.

From A HISTORY OF THE PEACE CONFERENCE OF PARIS
by H. W. V. Temperley (Oxford)

THE EUROPEAN GREAT POWERS AT THE OUTBREAK OF THE WAR

	Germany	Austria-Hungary	France	Great Britain	Russia	Italy
AREA (in sq. miles)	209,000	261,000	207,000	121,000	8,417,000	111,000
POPULATION (in millions, 1910)	64·9	51·4	39·2	45·2	163·7	34·7
STRENGTH OF ARMY	2,250,000	810,000	1,250,000	100,000	1,500,000	444,000
STRENGTH OF NAVY (capital ships)*	36	13	21	62	9	21
STEEL PRODUCTION (in thousand tons)	12,236	2,642	6,973	7,787	4,212	700
EXPENDITURE ON ARMAMENTS (in million dollars)	463	170	349	375	448	179

	Germany	Austria-Hungary	France	Great Britain	Russia	Italy
AREA* (in sq. miles)	182,000	—	213,000	†94,000	8,241,921	120,000
WAR DEATHS	1,855,000	1,457,000	1,325,000	744,000	1,700,000	563,000
WAR DEATHS AS PERCENTAGE OF MALES AGE 25–40	15·5	17·5	18·2	8·8	?	10·1
TOTAL CASUALTIES	‡7,143,000	7,020,000	6,161,000	2,441,673	9,150,000	2,197,000
NAVAL LOSSES (capital ships)	91	6	9	28	6	7
EXPENDITURE ON ARMAMENTS (in million dollars, 1930)	170	—	455	535	579	259

* These figures exclude dominions acquired by the Allied countries.
† This figure excludes Eire, which became a republic in 1921.
‡ These figures include dead, wounded and lost.

Books for Further Reading

Bennett, G.	*The Battle of Jutland*	Batsford 1964
Bishop, W. A.	*Winged Warfare*	Hodder 1918
Breach, R. W.	*Documents and Descriptions : the World since 1914*	Oxford University Press 1966
Bryant, A.	*English Saga 1840–1940*	Collins 1940
Cameron, J.	*1914*	Cassell 1959
Cameron, J.	*1916 : Year of Decision*	Oldbourne 1962
Churchill, W. S.	*The Great War*	Newnes 1934
Churchill, W.S.	*The World Crisis*	Mentor
Clarke, A.	*The Donkeys*	Hutchinson 1961
Gibbons and Morrican	*World War One*	Longman 1965
Gilbert, M.	*The European Powers 1900–45*	Weidenfeld & Nicolson 1965
Legg, S.	*Jutland : an Eyewitness Account*	Hart–Davis 1966
Macmillan, N.	*Into the Blue*	Jarrolds 1969
Markwick, A.	*The Deluge*	Bodley Head 1964
Masters, J.	*Fourteen Eighteen*	Joseph and Corgi 1965
Ogilvie, V.	*Our Times*	Batsford 1953
Pelling, H.	*Modern Britain*	Nelson and Sphere 1960
Seaman, L. C. B.	*Post Victorian Britain*	Methuen 1966
Taylor, A. J. P.	*English History 1914–45*	Oxford University Press 1965
Taylor, A. J. P.	*The First World War*	Penguin
Taylor, A. J. P.	*From Sarajevo to Potsdam*	Thames & Hudson 1966
Taylor, A. J. P.	*The Struggle for Mastery in Europe*	Oxford University Press 1954
Thompson, P. A.	*Lions Led by Donkeys*	Laurie 1929
Thoumin, R.	*The First World War*	Secker & Warburg 1963
Wells, H. G.	*The Outline of History*	Cassell 1961

Index